'Thought-pr
those interes
work will help build bridges between all those involved in raising
multilingual children.'

**Dr Muhammad Abdul Bari, educationalist,
author and parenting consultant**

'A many-layered exploration and celebration of the special role and value
of grandmothers for children as they grow and learn.'

Susan Langford MBE, Director, Magic Me

'What makes this book so unique is the way the author interweaves her
research findings with her own experiences as a young second generation
migrant who came to the UK at the age of nine. The study is infused by
her empathy with her participants, informed by her memories as a young
child upon her arrival in the UK, as a mother of young children and as a
daughter of her children's grandmother.'

**from the Foreword by Eve Gregory, Professor Emerita, Goldsmiths,
University of London**

Family Jigsaws

for Hamid, Tahseen, Mohseen, and Hasanat

Family Jigsaws

Grandmothers as the missing piece shaping bilingual children's learner identities

Mahera Ruby

 is an imprint of

First published in 2017 by the UCL Institute of Education Press, 20 Bedford Way, London WC1H 0AL

www.ucl-ioe-press.com

©2017 Mahera Ruby

British Library Cataloguing in Publication Data:
A catalogue record for this publication is available from the British Library

ISBNs
978-1-85856-783-9 (paperback)
978-1-85856-801-0 (PDF eBook)
978-1-85856-802-7 (ePub eBook)
978-1-85856-803-4 (Kindle eBook)

Every effort has been made to trace copyright holders and to obtain their permission for the use of copyright material. The publisher apologizes for any errors or omissions and would be grateful if notified of any corrections that should be incorporated in future reprints or editions of this book.

The opinions expressed in this publication are those of the author and do not necessarily reflect the views of the UCL Institute of Education.

Typeset by Quadrant Infotech (India) Pvt Ltd
Printed by CPI Group (UK) Ltd, Croydon, CR0 4YY
Cover by emc design ltd.

Contents

List of figures and tables

List of transcription symbols

I used the transcription codes used by Jefferson (1984) as a guide when transcribing the data from my study. The symbols used were not an attempt to represent everything as that would have been impossible. Rather, I selected some features that I identified as relevant and used those in the transcriptions.

(0.5)	Time gap (unfilled pauses)
(.)	Short pause in the talk
[ ]	Concurrent speech – overlapping talk
(( ))	Non-verbal activity or transcriber's comments on contextual or other features
!	Indicates an animated or emphatic (forceful) tone
( )	Empty parentheses indicate the presence of an unclear fragment on the tape
<u>Underscore</u>	Underlined fragments indicate speaker emphasis
CAPITALS	Words in capitals mark a section of speech noticeably louder than that surrounding it
°	Degree symbols are used to indicate that the talk they encompass is noticeably quieter than the surrounding talk
> <	'More than' and 'less than' symbols indicate that the talk they encompass was produced noticeably quicker than the surrounding talk
Italics	Bengali in the original
Bold	Translation of Bengali original

About the author

Mahera Ruby's Ph.D., completed in 2015, focuses on intergenerational learning in three-generation families originating in Bangladesh. She has a B.Sc. (Hons) in Chemistry, a PGCE in Secondary Science, and an M.Ed. Mahera is passionate about sharing her vibrant love of faith and community with her husband, their three sons, and her community. She has spent the best part of her life talking and listening to people in the community from all walks of life. This has led to a career as a researcher, personal development coach, and parenting coach.

Mahera has worked for the past decade as a researcher at Goldsmiths, University of London, using an ethnographic approach in the homes, communities, and classrooms of monolingual and bilingual children in East London. She co-directed the ESRC-funded research project on *Becoming Literate through Faith: Language and literacy learning in the lives of new Londoners*. She has also worked on research projects on developing bilingual pedagogies and has co-authored publications. As a research fellow, Mahera co-authored with Dr Charmian Kenner her first book, *Interconnecting Worlds: Teacher partnerships for bilingual learning*.

Mahera is a Trustee on the Board of the East London Mosque complex and an executive member of Tower Hamlets Citizens. She is involved in many interfaith projects, and coaches professionals, young people, parents, and individuals who are seeking to make changes and to maximize their strengths. She is keen to develop community leaders and vibrant community organizations.

Acknowledgements

This book would not have been possible without the help and support of many people.

I would like to thank Dr Charmian Kenner and Professor Eve Gregory for their guidance, wisdom, patience, and encouragement over the years, which helped me to keep going.

I am immensely grateful to the three families and two teachers who collaborated with me. I am indebted to them for sharing their stories with me and giving me their time, and I owe a particular debt of gratitude to the three children whose lively participation and learning processes motivated me to complete my journey so their voices could be heard.

I thank Gillian Klein for her editorial skills and belief in the book.

I would like to thank my friends, siblings and their spouses, and my nieces and nephews, who have always been there for me and supported me throughout this journey. Finally, I would like to extend my heartfelt love and gratitude to my parents; to my mother, who has not lived to see this accomplishment, but whose role as a mother and grandmother inspired me to embark on this journey, and to my father, whose unfailing faith in me gave me the perseverance to complete it.

> Thy Lord hath decreed that ye worship none but Him, and that ye be kind to parents. Whether one or both of them attain old age in thy life, say not to them a word of contempt, nor repel them, but address them in terms of honour. And, out of kindness, lower to them the wing of humility, and say: 'My Lord! Bestow on them thy Mercy even as they cherished me in childhood.'
>
> *Qur'ān*, Chapter 17: 23–4

Foreword

This study offers readers rare insights into the lives of three generations of three families whose origins lie in Bangladesh but who now live in East London. It investigates the complex nature of intergenerational relationships between grandparents, parents and young children as well as the perspectives of the children's teachers, and focuses upon the impact of these relationships on children's learning experiences at home and at school. What makes this book so unique is the way the author interweaves her research findings with her own experiences as a young second-generation migrant who came to the UK at the age of nine. The study is infused by her empathy with her participants, informed by her memories as a young child upon her arrival in the UK, as a mother of young children and as a daughter of her children's grandmother.

The author starts by unpicking the key terms that are crucial in her study – 'prolepsis', 'synergy', 'syncretism' and 'funds of knowledge' – and she explains these with special reference to bilingual children in the diaspora. She goes on to argue that children's learning cannot be compartmentalized, but takes place within a complex web of relationships that includes parents, grandparents and siblings as well as teachers. Chapters then unpick the differences between learning in each of the contexts above. Like the pieces of the jigsaw puzzles themselves that the author used as a research tool, we see how different chapters interlock to highlight the remarkable *flexibility* of young children as they negotiate their way through interactions with their mother, grandmother or teacher.

Existing studies tend to focus on *transgenerational learning*, whereby grandparents or older people pass down cultural, religious and linguistic knowledge to young children. In migratory contexts the older generation often has a wealth of knowledge to which young children otherwise have no access. However, this study unusually exemplifies *intergenerational learning* whereby an *exchange* rather than a simple transmission of learning takes place. Learning between the generations is mutual; grandparents teach the heritage language and culture to their grandchildren while at the same time learning new practices and skills from them. The scope and complexity of *intergenerational learning* will become increasingly apparent within an ageing and increasingly mobile population, and future studies will need to follow this to link research and practice. For example, in an increasingly mobile world, grandparents often cannot predict the future of their grandchildren and the concept of *prolepsis* becomes both problematic and exciting. Through this recognition, grandparents may begin to question preconceived ideas on what is possible in their own lives. Such exchanges as those in this book are truly intergenerational and provide an excellent example of work to emerge in the future from different communities in the UK and from across Europe.

Eve Gregory, Professor Emerita,
Goldsmiths, University of London

Introduction

Amar shomai ami tho eta phaisina, tara tho phora lekha khorsoin, hikhsoin amra tho shujug phaisina, tara aile ami golpo khoi, mati, kicha khoi ar khita hikhaimu? Ami tarar loge Bangla *mati tara o seshta khore matho. Amar loge khub bala thakhe ma aileo dushtami shuru oi, mare sethai, ma seshta khore, ashol oilogi ma babar lagi shonman thakhle shob oi, azkhar shomoi eta khom dekha zai.*

In my time I didn't get all this, they [her children] have studied, learned, we never had the opportunity, when they [grandchildren] come I tell them stories, folk tales, talk to them and what else should I teach them? I speak Bangla to them and they try to speak it. They are really good with me. They are good when they are with me, when mum comes they are naughty, they annoy their mum, actually if there is respect for dad and mum then all else is alright, nowadays there is less of that [respect].

Grandmother Sharma, Pilot study

This book is a journey born out of my own need to understand the lives of third-generation British-Bangladeshi children as learners who, like my own children, are in the middle of a web of intergenerational relationships within the home and at school. It is based on an ethnographic study that involved spending a lot of time with families at home and with their children at school. The experiences and multiple identities of three third-generation British-born Bangladeshi children, Aminah, Samiha, and Habib, who live in the East End of London, were investigated as they negotiated their learner identities with their mothers, grandmothers and teachers, while putting jigsaw puzzles together. It reveals for the first time the remarkable ability of these young bilingual children to be 'flexible learners' (Ruby, 2015) as they interacted at home with their grandmothers, Panna, Rekha, and Rahma (who often did not speak English), their mothers, Layla, Shamima, and Thamima, and their teachers, Jade and Hasna, at school. As Bateson (1979: 13) eloquently states, '[w]e come to every situation with stories, patterns and sequences of childhood experiences which are built into us. Our learning happens within the experience of what important others did'. This book explores and extends the accepted definitions of 'synergy'

(Gregory, 2001), 'prolepsis' (Cole, 1996) and 'syncretism' (Gregory and Williams, 2000) in intergenerational interactions, emphasizing the unique role of the grandmothers, and discusses the implications for all educators and policy-makers.

Many of you will already empathize with the struggles of being a young immigrant from a minority background living in a global city. Others will gain fresh insights and perspectives into the many complex and misunderstood issues affecting this social group and will apply such insights into policy, practice, and pedagogy. This book offers an appealing, modern, and syncretic version of learning based on rigorous research. It will take you through the jigsaw puzzles of these children's learning and illustrate the diversity, complexity, and attraction of intergenerational learning as a core component of what it means to be a third-generation British-Bangladeshi learner and the implications for the academic attainment of all bilingual schoolchildren.

I begin by summarizing the key conclusions, findings, and arguments of my doctoral study. I discuss why an ethnographic approach to research was chosen, my journey into research, the chosen activity, why I decided to investigate intergenerational learning and the complexities of being an insider/outsider as a researcher within my own community, and the issues this raised. I transcribed, transliterated, and translated all the audio and video data.

The key terms, prolepsis, synergy, syncretism, and funds of knowledge are introduced and defined at the beginning of chapter 2, in Part A, as they are important sociocultural learning constructs when investigating intergenerational influence in cross-cultural contexts, particularly with grandparents. In Part B, I go on to setting the context to intergenerational learning within communities, highlighting the history and background to the settlement of the Bangladeshi community in the East End of London, weaving in my own experiences as a migrant. In light of key research studies conducted in the past and those more current, learning in families across cultures and intergenerational learning in families are also explored. Chapter 2 concludes with an introduction to the interactions between Aminah, Samiha, and Habib with their respective grandmothers, Panna, Rekha, and Rahma, captured through a questionnaire.

Each immigrant has their own unique story to tell. Settling into a new country is not easy. It involves adapting to a new climate, new landscape, new language, new currency, and new lifestyle, all the while maintaining aspects of a previous culture and way of life. Throughout history, stories have been used to illuminate, to educate, to recount, to challenge and to engage.

Chapter 3 captures the personal voices, struggles, and successes of three grandmothers, Panna, Rekha, and Rahma, who moved to a new country. It shares how they negotiated their way through building a life for themselves and their children. It also captures the voices and stories of the mothers, Layla, Shamima, and Thaminah, the middle generation, as they try to integrate into British society and raise third-generation British-Bangladeshi children. It also introduces the many components of their complex identities.

Jade and Hasna are Aminah, Samiha, and Habib's class teachers. In chapter 4, the stories and the views of these two teachers are captured from their interview data. I explore the intergenerational interactions between the children and their teachers, the learning that takes place and how scaffolding (Wood *et al.*, 1976) is the construct that is most prominent during their joint endeavour of putting jigsaw puzzles together.

The journey continues in chapter 5, where I explain how the three 6-year-olds respond to their experiences of putting a jigsaw puzzle together at home with their mothers. It draws attention to the children's fascinating ability to engage by taking on new strategies to those they adopted when completing the puzzle with their teachers. Their interactions demonstrate how the way the learning is constructed leans towards guided participation (Rogoff, 1990). This is through exploring the nature of the verbal and non-verbal interactions as well as the turn-taking patterns exhibited during the puzzle activity between child and mother.

In chapter 6, the communicative purposes and functions of the grandmother and child's actions in relation to each other are captured, in contrast to those within the child–teacher and child–mother pairs. In the process of completing their tasks, the children show considerable learner flexibility (Ruby, 2015) in their interactions in order to understand the activity and their roles as learners. The role of the grandmothers is emphasized as the children negotiate their way through the different opportunities and demands that each situation presents. These are demonstrated through the following:

- turn-taking patterns
- language use
- children as teachers
- talk and the nature of partnerships.

Introduction

In chapter 7, learner flexibility and the implications for stakeholders in children's learning are discussed. Through the explorations and analysis carried out through chapters 4–6, it is possible to see how the concepts synergy, syncretizing of knowledge, prolepsis, and funds of knowledge from sociocultural theory apply to the intergenerational learning encounters. These webs of interactions are brought together in a diagram highlighting the strengths that currently exist in building children's learner identities. It also draws attention to the weaknesses that need to be addressed in order to recognize the incredible abilities of bilingual and multilingual children to be extremely resourceful in the strategies and choices they make and their ability to be flexible learners.

Chapter 1
Setting the foundation

I do try eh eh but where's the time? I don't seem to have enough hours in the day to keep up with everything ehm ... When Tahmid was little I did until he went to school, then it all disappeared and now with the younger ones its just easier and also [laughs] if I say anything to them in Bengali I've got to say it in English again anyway ... my mum's brilliant even though she can understand [English].

Rashida, mother

To my response, 'Really? Does she?' her answer was, 'yeah everything but she doesn't tell them that and they really try hard to speak to her'.

Rashida is a second-generation British-Bangladeshi mother. She was a part of the pilot study in my doctoral study, and her statement expresses the dilemmas of this second generation of mothers, their lack of time, and the important role the grandmothers play in the lives of their grandchildren. They tend to have more time, not only as carers, but as contributors to the children's learner identities. Her words also demonstrate how the family structures of bilingual and multilingual migrant families in the UK are changing. In the growing community of three-generation families, third-generation children speak English fluently and are doing well at school. Consequently, their bilingual skills are often overlooked. In the last half-century Britain has become not only ethnically and culturally diverse but also linguistically diverse, and we can expect the number of settlers who speak languages other than English to increase further still. The children of immigrants are now working here, and a significant number of them are teachers. But, like the children, they have seldom received recognition for their heritage languages. Often, bilingual teachers are themselves unsure about where they can utilize their linguistic and cultural funds of knowledge to enrich the learner identities of the bilingual children in their classrooms. This book shows that their languages can be used to enhance children's learning.

This chapter explains the journey I took as a researcher to conduct the study, which fills the gap in the field of intergenerational learning. The missing piece of the puzzle has been the role of grandparents in children's learning. I share the complexities of being a researcher in my own community and the need for this study in light of previous studies but also the need for it in the current context. The more I encountered families through the community, schools, and research projects, the more fascinated I became with the family dynamics within three-generation families. Questions began to form in my mind, ultimately leading to the research questions for my doctoral study: how do intergenerational relationships between grandparents, parents, and children impact on the learning that takes place between generations, and how does this contribute to the child's learning experiences at home and in school?

The children whose lives formed the basis of my doctoral study experienced different languages and cultures within their home and community settings. They grew up experiencing a web of interpersonal relationships with many adults and peers, each bringing their own experiences to building their funds of knowledge, which Moll (Cremin and Drury, 2015: 17) describes as 'the skills, strategies and information utilized by households, which may include information, ways of thinking and learning, approaches to learning and practical skills'.

These had an impact on the cognitive and social development of these children, as is recognized from a sociocultural perspective. Previously, psychologists have concentrated on methods of teaching and learning, while sociologists have focused on the economic disadvantages these children experience. Anthropologists and linguists investigate the cultural aspects of human society and the processes of communication all over the world. However, studies taking a sociocultural approach integrate the fields of developmental, cognitive, and cross-cultural psychology with those of cultural, social, and cognitive anthropology. A sociocultural approach, according to Gregory *et al.* (2004: 7), 'transcends academic disciplines and focuses on the inextricable link between culture and cognition through engagement in activities, tasks or events'.

However, there is little research and knowledge from a sociocultural perspective about how young third-generation bilingual children learn within three-generation families in the home. These children are in a unique position because they have the knowledge of their heritage culture from their grandparents and parents, as well as their knowledge of the mainstream English school culture from their parents and their own experience. This study contributes to and extends several key sociocultural learning concepts and constructs and their relevance to the learner identities of third-generation British-Bangladeshi children, namely: 'scaffolding' (Wood *et al.*, 1976); 'guided participation' (Rogoff, 1990); 'synergy' leading to mutual benefits for the young children and the adults (Gregory, 2001); 'syncretizing of knowledge' from different sources (Gregory and Williams, 2000); 'funds of knowledge' within communities (Moll, 1992); and the transmission of knowledge or 'prolepsis' between generations (Cole, 1996).

Journey into research

Questions of learner identities for third-generation British-Bangladeshi children are important, and I believe their learner identities have become more complex.

My curiosity about how personalities and identities are formed and my personal experiences and struggles with developing dual languages has driven me to learn more about the bilingual children in my classes. While on teacher training, I took the opportunity to shadow the home–school liaison officer to support some of the children exhibiting problem behaviours and attitudes. After several home visits and mentoring efforts, I gained a little insight into the lives of some of the students, noting the similarities to and differences from their parents and grandparents in their cultural, linguistic, psychological, and religious values, as well as the many gaps forming within the Bangladeshi community. These gaps seemed to cause a rift between the generations. I also noticed the frustrations of the monolingual trainee teachers when they delivered lessons to students they could not identify with. They struggled at times to communicate basic instructions across language and cultural barriers.

Upon becoming parents we, the second-generation mothers, began to notice that within three months of starting nursery our children's home languages began to disappear. This affected their relationship with members of their family who didn't speak English, particularly grandparents. A gap was opening between two generations who wanted and needed much from each other. I gained further insight into child development and how children learn during my MA in Education. I was fascinated by the different cultural practices around the world and how children function and learn in the social context within which they are reared.

My first academic encounter with research in this field was through the ESRC-funded research project by Kenner *et al.* (2004b) on *Intergenerational Learning between Children and Grandparents in East London*. The project explored the learning events that took place between the grandparents and their grandchildren, and the learning exchanges that occurred (Kenner *et al.*, 2004b; Kenner *et al.*, 2007; Ruby *et al.*, 2007; Kenner *et al.*, 2008; Gregory *et al.*, 2007). Both the children and the grandparents expressed the unique relationship they enjoyed and how this helped to promote intergenerational learning. The grandparents noted that they had time available and valuable funds of knowledge (Gonzáles *et al.*, 2005), which they utilized to build their relationship with their grandchildren.

I had the opportunity to observe the families in their home settings and see the interactions and dynamics between the members. Throughout the project I felt that one piece of the jigsaw was missing: the parents. During the home visits I became aware that the parent (usually the mother) was always kept out of the camera's range as the focus of the study was to investigate the learning interactions between grandparents and grandchildren. From my own experiences and the exposure I had to the families I could see the roles of various family members and became intrigued by the intricate and intertwined roles parents and grandparents played. I started to think about my own research interest in investigating the intergenerational learning interactions of the three generations. From the little literature available for this area it appeared that the dynamics of three-generation families had not been researched. More attention needs to be paid to children's learning experiences at home with both their parents and their grandparents.

People respond to their world differently; the task of research is complex and requires a methodology that is sensitive to such differences and complexities. Accordingly, I adopted an ethnographic approach using a sociocultural framework that allowed me to research complex situations by paying close attention to particular aspects, interactions, or phenomena in the setting without losing sight of the whole. Schieffelin and Ochs (1983: 48) define ethnographic descriptions as those 'that take into account the perspective of members of a social group, including beliefs and values that underlie and organize their activities and utterances'. One such dilemma was to fine-tune my role as a researcher who is an insider of the community being researched, but who needs to be an objective outsider.

The insider/outsider dilemma

Certain social, physical, and background-related factors contribute to a researcher being considered to be an insider or an outsider to the group s/he is researching. Fay's (1996) view is that being a member of the group being studied is neither necessary nor sufficient to being able to know the experience of that group. He outlined four reasons to support this stance. Firstly, individuals with their own experiences are unable to put the distance between them and the participants required to know where their experience is lacking, whereas someone from the outside may be adequately equipped to conceptualize the experience. Secondly, an insider can have confusing, ambivalent, mixed, and sometimes contradictory goals, motives, desires, thoughts, and feelings, whereas an outsider might be able to see through the complexity in ways the insider cannot. Thirdly, an outsider is often able to appreciate the wider perspective, with its connections, causal patterns, and influences. Finally, Fay proposed that we hide ourselves from ourselves out of fear, self-protection, and guilt and that it might be extremely difficult to disentangle ourselves.

When I reflected on and acknowledged my own reality and was aware of my own basic attributes, ideological assumptions, position of power within my culture, and my biases, all of them fundamental to the process of carrying out any research, I realized that my study did not fall within the traditional definition of ethnographic research. More and more natives are becoming authors of ethnographic studies investigating their own cultural group and writing about their own representations of the communities they study. Knowing how others see me and how I see the world can shape my research, but this also puts me in a position to protect the integrity of the research process. As Hammersley and Atkinson (1993) point out, as a social researcher doing a study within my own community I needed to remain faithful to the phenomena observed, taking into account my biases and subjectivities as a researcher, and protect the dignity and welfare of the researched.

Being a researcher allowed me to question my position within my own community in sharing an identity, language, and experiential base with my study participants (Asselin, 2003). I realized that being an insider enhanced the depth and breadth of my understanding. Questions about the objectivity, reflexivity, and authenticity of my research were raised by the participants and in my own mind. This was perhaps because I knew too much or was too close to the project and may have been too similar to those being studied (Kanuha, 2000: 444). This membership gave me a certain amount of legitimacy (Adler and Adler, 1987) and a readier acceptance by the participants. They were open with me and this brought greater depth to the data gathered. The participants were willing to share with me their experiences, both positive and negative, as they saw me as one of them, someone who understood them.

The school

All three children attended 'Dockside' School, which is situated near the Docklands to the east of the City of London. This area has a strong maritime character. Severely damaged during the Blitz, the area remained run down and derelict into the 1980s. It was then transferred to the management of the London Docklands Development Corporation, who were tasked with redeveloping the area. The London Docks were mainly redeveloped with various commercial, light industrial, and residential properties, where families from the surrounding neighbourhoods started to settle.

As the community grew, a new primary Dockside School opened in 1989 to augment the 65 primary schools in the borough. The attractive modern building of brick and Welsh slates is situated near St Katharine Docks, the River Thames, and the Tower of London, all three important tourist attractions, and is near Brick Lane and Canary Wharf. The single form entry school caters for children aged 3 to 11 years and has capacity for 360 pupils. Alongside classrooms and other key facilities, the school has a parent room that is well used. It has some unusual features for a city school, such as a nature reserve and a pond. Unlike other non-denominational schools in the borough, it has a diverse intake of pupils. The area has only recently begun to develop residential properties, so the school has a low intake from its immediate catchment area. Most of the pupils live locally but the school attracts children from all over the borough. Some are European families who have temporarily moved into the area due to their work commitments and others are from the indigenous white and Bangladeshi families.

The puzzle activity

I set up an activity in which the children, their teachers, mothers, and grandmothers put together jigsaw puzzles. It seemed a good way for me to observe interactions between the participants with as little interruption as possible. Using the puzzles required the child to focus on a specific task with the help of a particular adult. The jigsaw puzzles were chosen because they were portable and similar to the computer activity staged in the study by Kenner *et al.* (2008), which had demonstrated that such an activity could be naturalistic even though it was staged. Puzzles are generally acknowledged as a learning tool to aid cognitive and social development (Isaacson, 2010).

The task-based activity encouraged the families to play and exchange knowledge and expertise. Putting a puzzle together is an informal activity that can be seen as play. Vygotsky (1978) concluded that play has two critical qualities that, when combined, can contribute to development. First, representational play creates an imaginary situation that permits the child to deal with unrealizable desires, a way of deferring immediate gratification. Second, play contains rules for behaviour that children must follow if they are to succeed. Vygotsky was referring to fantasy play, but putting a puzzle together supported and broadened the linguistic skills required to develop and express different points of view, resolve disagreements, and persuade peers to collaborate so play can continue.

Play offers an arena in which all facets of conversational dialogue can be extended, including questioning. In sum, Vygotsky (1978: 62) stated that fantasy play contributes to social maturity and to the construction of diverse aspects of cognition, such as positive overall intellectual performance, the generation of creative ideas, memory for diverse forms of information, language competence, the capacity to reason theoretically, the differentiation of appearance and reality, and the playful stream of verbal narrative that comments on and assists us in coping with our daily lives. The children collaborated with their mothers, grandmothers, and teachers during the informal activity of putting the puzzles together, generating creative ideas and developing the children's language and learning.

The four jigsaw puzzles the children and adults put together were:

- Puzzle 1: UK and the Republic of Ireland Map
  Suitable for ages 4–10. A 100-piece puzzle featuring places of interest from around the United Kingdom and Ireland.
- Puzzle 2: Jungle Floor Puzzle
  Suitable for ages 3–6. A 24-piece puzzle featuring a friendly cartoon jungle scene with lots of creatures to spot.
- Puzzle 3: Solar System
  Suitable for ages 4–8. A 60-piece puzzle to help learn the names of the planets in the solar system.
- Puzzle 4: Endangered Species
  Suitable for ages 3–8. A 53-piece puzzle featuring endangered animals from around the world.

The puzzles were all very colourful. Each showed a large picture of the completed puzzle on the front of the box and smaller pictures on the back. On the boxes of puzzles 3 and 4 there was information about the planets or the endangered animals featured in the puzzle.

The next chapter is in two parts. Part A begins by defining the sociocultural learning concepts in intergenerational learning. In Part B, the historical context to the settlement of the Bangladeshi community is set, going on to exploring the nature of learning taking place within families. The chapter concludes by giving an introduction to the interactions between Aminah, Samiha, and Habib with their respective grandmothers, Panna, Rekha, and Rahma.

Chapter 2
Intergenerational learning

Part A

Before looking at how intergenerational learning has evolved over time, it is helpful to define the sociocultural learning constructs, prolepsis, synergy, syncretism, and funds of knowledge that affect intergenerational influence in cross-cultural contexts, particularly with grandparents.

Prolepsis

Cole (1996) identifies the transmission of knowledge between members of different generations as the process of prolepsis. It is a kind of intergenerational link that can be interesting to observe if both participants in the learning event are generations apart and the older participant is a migrant. Cole puts forward a sociocultural explanation of the cultural mediation of development whereby prolepsis is 'the cultural mechanism that brings the end into the beginning' (183). Gregory *et al.* explain this further:

> The adult brings her idealized memory of her cultural past and her assumption of cultural continuity in the future to actual interactions with the child in the present. In this non-linear process, the child's experience is both energized and constrained by what adults remember of their own pasts and imagine what the child's future will be.
>
> Gregory *et al.*, 2004: 10

The grandparents, Rahma, Panna, and Rekha, have been raised in Bangladesh and have settled in a new country. They shared these experiences with their grandchildren during the puzzle activity. It was clear that the children explored interdependence and 'linked lives' as the children learned with their mothers and grandmothers, but did not when they were interacting with their teachers.

Synergy

Grandparents and grandchildren hold a similar place in society based essentially on their sense of vulnerability at either end of the spectrum of age (Kenner *et al.*, 2004a). This sense of vulnerability gives rise to a unique relationship of mutuality (Kenner *et al.*, 2007). It relates to Gregory's

(2001) research on siblings, which looks beyond the existing terminologies of scaffolding, guided participation, or collaborative learning to 'synergy', which she explains as 'a unique reciprocity whereby siblings act as adjuvants in each other's learning, i.e. older children teach younger siblings and at the same time develop their own learning' (309).

Gregory maintains that, in contrast, the terms 'scaffolding' and 'guided participation' indicate 'an unequal relationship between participants in that learning is unidirectional from the older or more experienced person to the younger child' (303). She argues that the children were able to construct their learning powerfully at home because 'synergy is the key mediator through which knowledge ... is internalised' (311), whereas at school bilingual children are 'faced with the effects of being unable to communicate in a context they do not yet understand and in which they are not at ease' (45).

Interactions with grandparents and grandchildren around the computer described by Kenner *et al.* (2008) demonstrated synergy in action. The younger generation had greater facility in operating the computer, which was a new cultural artefact for the grandmothers, while the older generation were more experienced in literacy and other areas of learning, so both parties had knowledge to share. The children were more familiar with the technical language of computers and the grandparents more competent in the family's first language, so again the dynamics of the interaction demonstrated the synergy taking place, with both learning from the other while able to utilize their areas of expertise. This concept of synergy applied to Rekha, Rahma, and Panna, as each brought particular expertise to the task of putting a puzzle together.

Syncretism

As people start to integrate into the host society, cultures begin to blend and evolve. Kulick (1992) uses the term syncretism to describe the creative transformation of culture. Apter (1991) understood it to be more than a mixing of existing cultural forms. It is instead, as seen by Shaw and Stewart (1994), a creative process where culture is reinvented by people as they draw on familiar and new resources, bringing to life 'mundane practices of everyday life' (Rosaldo, 1993: 217). The concept of syncretism has been extended by Duranti and Ochs (1997: 173) 'to include hybrid cultural constructions of speech acts and speech activities that constitute literacy'. These authors define syncretic literacy as 'an intermingling or merging of culturally diverse traditions that informs and organizes literacy activities' (72).

According to Kenner *et al.* (2004b), children do not remain in separate worlds but acquire membership of different groups simultaneously, i.e. they live in 'simultaneous worlds'. They often syncretize the languages, literacies, narrative styles, and role relationships appropriate to each group, and then go on to transform the languages and cultures they use to create new forms that are relevant to their purposes. The puzzle activity between the children and their mothers and grandmothers afforded many opportunities for syncretic interactions, as the participants brought a variety of experiences to the activity that blended during their interactions.

Funds of knowledge

The notion of funds of knowledge (Moll, 1992) is of importance within intergenerational learning at home and in school. The cultural deficit model stemmed from negative beliefs and assumptions about the ability, aspirations, and work ethic of marginalized people. The assertion was that students of colour and those from low-income families often fail to do well in school because of perceived cultural deprivation or lack of knowledge of the cultural models compatible with school success. According to Bourdieu (1977), such students consequently enter school lacking the kind of the cultural capital that is affirmed by schools and shared by school agents and thus considered valuable. In addition, an assumption may persist that children from ethnic minorities and the families of students from socio-economically disadvantaged backgrounds do not value education in the same way as their middle- and upper-class white counterparts do. According to the theory, upper- and middle-class children are more likely to do well in school because they possess more cultural capital. However, Moll *et al.* (2001) argue that all families possess funds of knowledge, which they define as the '[h]istorically accumulated and culturally developed bodies of knowledge and skills essential for household or individual functioning and well-being' (133).

These authors maintain that teachers can only come to know their students and their families if they can put aside their role of teacher and expert and take on a role of learner. Cremin *et al.* (2015) furthered the idea of the teacher as being a learner through conducting 'Learner Visits' during the BC:RLL project. During home visits, the teachers gained new knowledge of the rich cultural, linguistic, and social assets present in households and that children bring to school. By increasing their awareness of community and family funds of knowledge, the teachers understood parental participation as 'an open-ended and multifaceted activity' (Moll and Cammarota, 2010: 304). The teachers were able to use this knowledge in their classroom and facilitate new opportunities for learning, thus 'fostering a two-way traffic between home and school' (Mottram and Powell, 2015: 144). The teachers became insiders in their pupils' social worlds and cultures' (Cremin and Collins, 2015).

Part B

Mone ase ya Allah *ek bare andar!* Christmas'*e ashsilam, snow khita silo gho* airport'*e eshe dekhi* snow *ekbare kono gaas'e patha nai thea ami kotho shomoi phore boli 'ei desher patha ki zou kisu khae nise?'*

I remember yes Allah **it was totally dark! Came during** Christmas, **oh there was not just** snow, **when I came to the** airport **I just saw** snow **and there were absolutely no leaves on the trees, after a while I asked 'did something eat all the leaves of this country?'**

Rahma, Habib's grandmother

She reminisced further about her first reaction to the house she was to live in:

… furana ghore silam ami ghor dekhei ami bolsilam 'na ami ei deshe thakhbona ei deshe kono gusul korar bebosta nai ami thakbo na ami sole zabo', tho uni bole 'tumi ki rokom zaba?' 'Tho Bethnal Green *dia tho* bus *zai ami bolsi oi* bus'*e ute sole zabo.'*

… stayed in an old house, after I saw the house, I said 'I don't want to stay in this country, there aren't any facilities to have a wash I will not stay I want to go', so he [husband] said 'how will you go?' So I said 'the bus **that goes through** Bethnal Green **I will get on that and go'.**

Rahma

Every migrant has a story and every migrant community has a historical context. The snapshot from this interview with Rahma reveals her distress at arriving in a new country and her urge to go back to what she was familiar with. The families in my research are part of a community who came with very young families. Their families have grown, often settling near one another or living within the same household, creating levels of intergenerational relationships. In this chapter, these relationships are explored to highlight the nature of learning interactions that exist within the home.

The Borough of Tower Hamlets in London is known for being welcoming to new migrant communities. Located east of the City of

London and north of the River Thames, it covers most of the East End of London. By 1891, Tower Hamlets was already one of the most populated areas in London and successive waves of foreign immigration added to the existing overcrowding and poverty. This rich history of immigration began with Huguenot refugees, who settled in Spitalfields in the seventeenth century, followed by Irish weavers, Ashkenazi Jews and, in the twentieth century, Bangladeshis. The first Bangladeshis to migrate to the UK in the early 1900s were seamen who were often ship's cooks. Economic hardship in East Pakistan in the 1950s and 1960s, coupled with labour shortages in the UK, saw an influx of migrant Bangladeshi workers, most of whom settled in Tower Hamlets and in Birmingham. During the Bangladesh War of Independence in 1971, a large number of men, mostly from the area of Sylhet, migrated to London for work and to escape political instability. The late 1960s saw rapid population expansion, as families from Bangladesh joined those already in the UK. This migration brought cultural and religious enrichment, particularly in food, music, arts, literature, drama, and more recently festivals in East London.

I am a second-generation, bilingual, British-Bangladeshi, raising third-generation British-Bangladeshi children. Like many other families, we travelled from Bangladesh to join our father in the UK. We arrived in February 1980, a difficult time for us, particularly for my mother, who shared a similar experience to the one Rahma describes, as well as for my older siblings, who bore the full impact of the move as we had no family in the UK. The movement from one social context to another was accompanied by intense feelings of psychological dislocation. We all suffered a sense of profound loss over leaving our homeland and the pangs of adapting to a new society. The disorientation following arrival, the trauma of resettlement and the problems of acculturation hit us all. My mother was hit particularly hard, because she had to leave my very elderly grandfather for whom she had been the sole carer and who had taught her all she knew since she moved into the family home when she was 15.

In the 1980s, many men and women from the Bangladeshi community worked in the garment industry. The availability of semi-skilled and unskilled labour led to low wages and poor conditions throughout the East End and as each group of immigrants became more financially secure, they tended to move to more affluent areas. As communities settle and families grow, the learning and child-rearing practices within families and communities are 'constantly in the process of change as the London community shapes itself to changing pressures and demands' (Mahon, 1997: 29). This naturally has an impact on the intergenerational interactions between family members.

Researchers and educators have long paid attention to the ways in which children learn and develop. For many, the social context – in other words, the varied surroundings of home, school, and community where children learn to talk, read, write, and socialize – has been of particular interest. Wells stresses that:

> ... children are not only influenced by the social context in which they develop, but their very development as humans is dependent on opportunities to participate with others, notably parents, family members, peers and teachers, in the activities that constitute the culture in which they are growing up.
>
> Wells, 2009: 271

Thus, a child's learning and development is as much a social achievement as it is an individual one.

Similarly, my mother was anxious about the context in which she was raising us. She constantly worried about our safety because of racism and anti-social behaviour in our area. The fear of settling in a foreign country was difficult enough, but having to adjust to living amongst people of different cultures and values proved to be quite challenging for us all. We were apprehensive about going out and feared being hurt, which drove my mother to keep us mostly at home. I would also hear my parents late into the night discussing how they would cope and would hear my father reassuring my mother. They would spend time reminiscing about the life she had left behind. There were times when I saw her brushing away tears and heard her muffled sobs when she thought we were fast asleep.

At the age of 8, on the first day at school, which was across the road from where we lived, I had my first intimate experience of English culture: its food, people, and language. I was the kid in class who couldn't speak English, had brown skin, and wore a headscarf. This was not a common sight in the 1980s, particularly the headscarf. My sister and I were the only girls in our neighbourhood and at school who dressed this way. The earliest memories I have of school and the community are of not fitting in. All the other children conversed in English and the Bangladeshi children spoke in another dialect of Bengali to ours: Sylheti. Sylheti is an oral language spoken by most families in our East London community who came from Sylhet, a north-eastern area in Bangladesh. It was difficult for me to understand this dialect, as we are from another part of Bangladesh and speak the standard Bengali, the form used in writing. Looking back, I realize that I made every effort to assimilate but found it difficult, as I felt I was different to the Bangladeshi children because I didn't speak as they did and didn't quite identify culturally with children from other ethnic backgrounds. My efforts to merge into the mainstream environment meant speaking only English and leaving cultural norms for when I got home and interacted with my parents and siblings. Being an emerging bilingual brought with it other issues.

Bilingual and multilingual issues

No special provisions appear to have been made in the UK for South Asian children in state schools until the 1960s, when the British government began looking more closely at the issue. By the time Bangladeshi children arrived, the idea of mother-tongue teaching in community classes had begun to gain ground and was eventually introduced in some secondary schools in areas of high Bangladeshi population such as Tower Hamlets. In school, EAL (English as an Additional Language) classes were set up for bilingual children to learn English. To attend these classes, the children had to leave their mainstream lessons. I for one strongly resented this idea because I felt alienated and was made to feel different from the others.

Bilingual children encounter particular issues. As Cummins (1996, 2006) stressed, language is linked with cultural identity, and bilingual learning can increase the self-esteem of bilingual children, which can in turn support educational achievement. Most of the studies investigating bilingual learning have been conducted in countries providing mainstream bilingual education, often with first-generation children. Educators including Edwards (1998) and Smyth (2003) have also recommended using the home language as a resource in schools that educate through the dominant language, to enable the children to build on their prior knowledge and have better access to curriculum content. However, there is research indicating that bilingual children have additional issues that affect their development at school because their learning at home is not taken into account.

Home for me presented an environment with a different kind of learning alongside the academic. In the social world in and around my family, I knew where my place was; elders and youngsters were clearly defined by the ways I addressed them. My siblings and I were given precise instructions as to how we conducted ourselves with one another, as well as with adults and guests. I could be challenging at times, but I certainly knew my boundaries. At home, I felt secure and content, but was frustrated when I left the comfort of my family and Bangladeshi community and could not share these practices. Did I have to adapt, adopt, and transform my ways so that I could blend in with those who questioned my dress and cultural norms? How far would I have to go before I was accepted? It affected me emotionally at times when the very teachers I hoped would educate the ignorant failed to accept my values.

I refused to leave my class to join the EAL classes. By staying in the classroom with all the children and with the loving support of my class teacher, I picked up English within three months. At home, my mother maintained a tight regime of keeping our Bengali intact by making us read Bengali books and newspapers, write regularly, and not allowing us to speak English at home. My mother's storytelling, in a language only my home setting recognized, always unleashed happy emotions. I felt I still spoke that language in my sleep, in my dreams, evocative of a country I had left but which also sounded like the only home I had ever known. The stories made me realize that there was a corner of me that would forever not be English. I had the ability to think in two languages, and each compensated for the other when I struggled to understand or express myself.

Drury (2007) highlights some of these issues in her ethnographic study. Her findings offer significant insights into the experiences of 3- and 4-year-old bilingual children as they begin school in three different English nursery classes. Drury raises the issue of the difference between home and school, highlighting the important aspects of children's learning that took place in the home that were still unrecognized in nursery school. Drury refers to these aspects as 'invisible learning', showing the children were confident in their use of the two languages at home, and constantly code-switching to gain control of situations involving adults as well as children.

Drury also challenged the low expectations teachers have of bilingual children and their experiences of learning in the home, contrasting it with the high aspirations of the parents. She suggested that home–school understandings can be developed through contact with children and their families. While I was growing up, I felt there was an assumption among teachers that cultural and language barriers hinder bilingual children's ability to achieve. At times it bothered me a great deal to observe the low expectations teachers held of us. I resented how it was always assumed that our parents didn't care about our education, because some did not attend parents' evenings. If only they could come to our homes and see the efforts our parents made to support us in taking up the opportunities they never had! If only I could tell them that the respect and honour we showed towards the teachers were taught to us by our parents! These parents were never part of a system of education they could play a role in. The policies for home–school links seemed encouraging, but in practice the school gates were where parents handed us over to experts who knew how to teach us.

Teachers holding negative and sometimes culturally determined views about the children they teach were studied by Kenner *et al.* (2007). They quote, for example, a teacher who suggests that most of the Bangladeshi parents were not active in their children's learning at home, since few had walked with their children on Tower Bridge or taken them to visit the Tower of London and the museums. In the teacher's view, this demonstrated that these parents had failed to embrace British culture and values and were not serious about their children's education. Such a perception raises the question of what constitutes learning and highlights the need to investigate the importance of learner identities of third-generation British-Bangladeshi children at home.

Learning in families across cultures

Cross-cultural studies of children's socialization and its influence on their development have been mainly carried out by researchers immersing themselves within the communities they study. Ethnographic studies from the fields of psychology and anthropology have focused for the most part on the cultural worlds of early childhood and children's language socialization (Harkness, 1975; Harkness and Super, 1977; Heath, 1983; Schieffelin and Ochs, 1986a and b). These studies have drawn findings from cross-cultural community contexts concerning parent–child interactions within different cultures and subcultures, attempting to gauge the influence of cultural practices on cognitive development and language learning. For example, Schieffelin and Ochs (1983) compare observations of middle-class British and American nuclear families with the Kaluli people of Papua New Guinea. In both communities, the process socialized the child 'into culturally specified models of organizing knowledge, thought and language' (53). The children from the middle-class families learned who could interpret their utterances and how to express agreement or disagreement through the way the caregivers offered successive possible interpretations of a child's utterance. On the other hand, the Kaluli children learned to be assertive through the use of particular linguistic expressions and verbal sequences modelled to them by their mothers. Their socialization took place through participation in two, three, and multiparty social interactions.

In the 1980s, most Bangladeshi children in the East End of London were encouraged by their parents to attend Qur'ān and language classes outside school, often in the evenings, five days a week, and some attended Bengali classes during the weekend. Many of these classes took place in the living rooms of homes in the neighbourhood. The home life of many Bangladeshi families in Britain emphasized links with the homeland. The parents' generation spoke in their mother tongue, regularly attended mosque, watched Bollywood films, and made family trips back to Bangladesh. My parents used to wait eagerly for the newspapers from Bangladesh to arrive in the post. They would huddle around them for hours, catching up with events back home and then listen to us reading the news items out loud to them. But the second generation began to find their own cultural niche, a fusion of West with East. I remember the teachers being very critical and concerned about the extended routine of study these children had to follow. Some children were taught at home; I was taught to read the Qur'ān and Bengali at home by my parents and older siblings, a learning that my teachers knew little about.

While my mother ardently kept up our Bengali, we were exposed to English and Arabic at home through the personal example of my father. He would recite from the Qur'ān after the dawn prayers and then listen to the news on the radio while walking up and down the passage, knocking at each of our rooms to wake us up for morning prayers. We didn't have a television, but my earliest memories from childhood are of the deep voices of the newsreaders from the World Service, and of listening to the afternoon plays on BBC Radio 4. My elder sister and I used to wait eagerly for the publications *Reader's Digest* and *Mahjuba* (a women's magazine from Iran) to come by post every month, and I remember spending many a summer holiday copying out the stories and doing my own illustrations to go with them.

I am a second-generation mother with mixed cultural experiences at home and at school, different to those of my mother who migrated to the UK from Bangladesh. This has had an impact on my children's cultural upbringing and experiences of living in the UK and on their interactions with their grandparents. The children's languages also play a part in their interactions at home and at school. The second- and third-generation 7–11-year-olds in Kenner *et al.*'s (2008) study, mostly fluent in English, were attending after-school community classes where they studied Bengali, their mother tongue. This study investigated how the children at primary schools in East London would respond to using Bengali as well as English for learning in their classrooms where English is usually the only language.

The findings from the research were revealing. Although the children were fluent in English and were mostly high achievers, they considered their mother tongue to be a key aspect of their identity and wished to use both Bengali and English for learning in the mainstream classroom. Kenner and her colleagues found that bilingual activities enhanced the children's learning – as was demonstrated when children discovered that they could deal with concepts, such as metaphors, similes, and mathematical constructs, by being able to use one language to aid understanding in another. Translating required the children to reformulate ideas, thus enriching their learning and increasing their metalinguistic awareness, giving them the chance to use and extend their bicultural knowledge. The study also revealed that unless children received the required support to develop their mother tongue, they were in danger of losing these skills and abilities.

This is where Brice Heath's (1983) ethnographic study exploring the differences between children's acquisition of language at home and at school is so telling. She looked at three different communities within the Piedmont area of the Carolinas: Trackton, a black working-class mill community of rural origin; Roadville, a white working-class mill community of Appalachian origin; and Maintown, representing mainstream, middle-class, school-oriented culture. Each community had strikingly different language socialization patterns (Heath, 1982). She studied children's language development focusing on literacy events such as bedtime story reading. Although bedtime stories didn't take place in Trackton or Roadville, both were literate communities and the children went to school with certain expectations of print and believed that through reading they would learn things they needed to know (Heath, 1980). In both Trackton and Roadville, the children were unsuccessful in school yet both communities placed a high value on achieving well at school.

Tellingly, Heath found crucial differences in the ways children and adults interacted with one another in Trackton and Roadville during pre-school years and how each differed from the interactions in Maintown. In Trackton, children 'learn to talk', whereas in Roadville adults 'teach them how to talk' (57). Roadville children were taught how to talk by being exposed to literacy through many visual stimuli such as colourful, decorative pictures and text on the walls. Book reading focused on letters of the alphabet, numbers, pictures, and the retelling of stories in the words of the adult. Carers asked questions and provided simplified explanations for children's what–questions. These children tended to do well in their initial years at school but during later years struggled with thinking for themselves and could rarely provide personal commentary on real or book stories.

On the other hand, the children in Trackton learned to talk by coming home to an environment where there was a lot of human contact and communication, both verbal and non-verbal. There were no reading materials aimed at the children, so their literacy exposure was through newspapers, mail, calendars and circulars, school material sent home to parents, and church-related materials. The children were not read to and had no bedtime stories but were surrounded by different kinds of social interactions.

Intergenerational learning in families

Studies of intergenerational interaction can be found in diverse fields, from psychology to medicine to public policy. However, none to date have researched the significant role of intergenerational interaction between three-generation families in the extended family structure. The role of grandparents in the lives of their grandchildren has generally been underestimated, particularly with regard to children's learning. Grandparents are taking on an increasing role in childcare, generally through choice but sometimes because there is no option. If we look at some of the facts about the role grandparents play in the UK, it becomes clear that it is an area of support to the family that has gone unnoticed for too long. According to the Basic Skills Agency (BSA, 2007), there are approximately 13 million grandparents in the UK. In the past two generations, the number of children cared for by grandparents has jumped from 33 per cent to 82 per cent. More than a third of grandparents spend the equivalent of three days a week caring for their grandchildren. The contribution of grandparents to children's learning is therefore a crucial area of research. Despite these important demographic trends, grandparent–grandchild relationships have rarely been studied within education.

The complexity of three-generational or multi-generational relationships was addressed by Williams and Nussbaum:

> The simple dyad of parent-child or grandparent-grandchild operating in an interactive vacuum without being affected by various other intergenerational relationships occurring around them is a convenient but rather simplistic way to begin the study of such relationships – it is not reality. Families increasingly consist of several levels of intergenerational interaction affecting each other in complex and hitherto underexplored ways.
>
> Williams and Nussbaum, 2001: 184

King *et al.* (1998) refer to these overlapping ecological contexts of the three-generational family as 'linked lives', the grandparents, parents, and grandchildren carrying out their individual life courses within interdependent intergenerational relationships. Grandparents' and grandchildren's interactions and relationships are often mediated by parents, both directly through the parents' efforts to increase or decrease contact and indirectly through the way parents interact with their own parents and create an environment for their children's access to their grandparents (King and Elder, 1995). The mothers in this book were also the mediators for setting up contact between the children and their grandmothers, as well as my access to them. The mothers all live busy lives and contact depends on them organizing the visits. I was keen to see the linked lives of these families and the layers of relationships and interdependence that existed between them.

Smith (1995) drew together research findings on the psychology of grandparenthood that spanned almost half a century, from 1957 to 2000. He put forward different studies that covered issues around grandparenthood, some of which I highlight here as relevant to this book. In the early studies, grandmothers particularly were portrayed as problematic in childrearing. Vollmer (1937: 382) reiterates this view, saying that 'the practical conclusion is that the grandmother is not a suitable custodian of the care and rearing of her grandchild; she is a disturbing factor against which we are obliged to protect the child according to the best of our ability'. However, from the 1960s on, grandparents are presented more favourably. The change in the attitudes and roles of grandparents started to take place when some of them began seeing themselves as 'reservoirs of family wisdom' (Neugarten and Weinstein, 1964). Certain researchers worried that grandparents were becoming more remote and detached and that this would weaken the 'vital connection of grandparents and grandchildren' (Kornhaber and Woodward, 1981). Others emphasized the importance of grandparents as support and socialization agents (Tinsley and Parke, 1984), even though this only applied to a small proportion of their sample.

The funds of knowledge on which children can draw have been highlighted by the findings in Kenner *et al.*'s (2004a) research on intergenerational learning between children and grandparents in East London. The researchers worked with small groups of Bangladeshi, Anglo-English and black and minority ethnic grandparents and their grandchildren of primary-school age. Kenner *et al.* (see also Gregory *et al.*, 2007; Ruby *et al.*, 2007) have highlighted that intergenerational home-based learning can be advantageous for schools, what Moll *et al.* (2013) call 'informal learning'.

In Kenner *et al.*'s (2004b) study not only were the informal activities such as cooking, gardening, storytelling, reading, and shopping viewed as enjoyable activities by the grandchildren, but they also provided important intergenerational learning opportunities. It was particularly apparent with the Bangladeshi and African-Caribbean grandparents that sharing cultural, religious, historical, and linguistically-based knowledge with grandchildren was valued. These activities also developed transferable skills that could be used in the classroom, as they fulfilled aspects of curriculum learning. For example, reading skills were attained via stories, and numeracy skills via shopping and cooking. In addition, reciprocal learning was visible, with grandchildren teaching grandparents new skills, such as in IT. The grandparents also passed on linguistic and cultural knowledge, strengthening the child's language and literacy levels by reciting poems, reading stories, and writing.

A similar questionnaire was conducted with Panna, Rekha, and Rahma as one of the initial activities. Table 2.1 overleaf is a summary of the activities the grandmother–grandchild pair engaged in.

Table 2.1 shows that the three grandmothers interacted with their grandchildren in Bengali and English during most of the activities. The order of the languages indicate how much they were used in each one. In some activities, Arabic was used, such as during religious activities (6), for singing and rhymes together (11) and for school work (12), which in this case included helping the children with their Quranic class and weekend Islamic School work. When they watched TV/videos (14) together, some spoke Hindi, as both Rekha and Panna liked to watch Hindi films with their grandchildren. Interestingly, none of the grandmothers ate out (5) with their grandchildren and neither were they involved in any sports activities (19) with them. As none of them lived with their grandchildren, they were not involved in getting the children ready for school (16).

All three grandmothers enjoyed taking their grandchildren shopping (1), usually to the local street market to buy toys, cooking utensils, and Asian vegetables from the stalls. The children enjoyed taking part in cooking (2) by helping to peel garlic/ginger and chopping vegetables. Rekha liked to encourage Samiha to help prepare the table before meals. Aminah liked to help her grandmother with weeding her garden (3) and Habib was keen to help Rahma on her allotment at the local city farm where they grew lots of Bangladeshi vegetables. As Rekha lived in a flat, this opportunity was not freely available for Samiha. But video data from the *Grandparents Project* (Kenner *et al.*, 2004) did capture her doing a lot of gardening with her paternal grandmother. Rekha tried to get Aminah to help her around the house (4) doing little jobs. All three spent time encouraging their grandchildren to help their parents with their household chores. They advised them and tried to teach them the importance of pleasing their parents as a way of gaining reward from God.

Table 2.1: Questionnaire summary for grandmother–grandchild pair (the ticks indicate the main language used)

	Activity	Name of child, grandmother, activities & language used		
		Aminah/Panna	Samiha/Rekha	Habib/Rahma
1.	Shopping	✓Bengali & English	✓Bengali & English	✓Bengali & English
2.	Cooking	✓Bengali & English	✓Bengali	✓Bengali & English
3.	Gardening	✓Bengali & English		✓Bengali
4.	Doing housework with them	✓Bengali & English	✓Bengali & English	✓Bengali & English
5.	Eating out			
6.	Religious activities	✓Bengali, English & Arabic	✓Bengali & Arabic	✓Bengali, English & Arabic
7.	Reading	✓English	✓Bengali	✓Bengali & English
8.	Telling stories	✓Bengali	✓Bengali	✓Bengali
9.	Visiting others	✓Bengali & English	✓Bengali	✓Bengali & English
10.	Talking about members of the family and family history	✓Bengali & English	✓Bengali	✓Bengali
11.	Singing & rhymes together		✓Bengali & English	✓English & Arabic
12.	Doing school work with them	✓Bengali & English		✓Arabic
13.	Computer activities	✓Bengali & English		✓Bengali & English
14.	Watching TV/ videos	✓Bengali, English & Hindi	✓Bengali, English & Hindi	✓Bengali & English

	Activity	Name of child, grandmother, activities & language used		
		Aminah/Panna	Samiha/Rekha	Habib/Rahma
15.	Playing	✓Bengali & English	✓Bengali & English	✓Bengali & English
16.	Getting them ready for school			
17.	Taking them to school			✓Bengali & English
18.	Going to the park			✓Bengali & English
19.	Sports			
20.	Other			

Rekha liked to read the Qur'ān with Samiha and recite *surahs* (chapters from the Qur'ān) and *duas* (prayers) with her from memory (6). Rekha and Samiha sometimes listened to recitations on audio tapes and the TV by well-known reciters from across the world and read verses from the Qur'ān together. Habib and Rahma prayed some of their daily prayers together, generally in Arabic. Habib attended the mosque with Rahma on most winter weekdays on the way back from school, as Rahma liked to catch the late-afternoon prayer before going home. All three women felt it was important to teach their grandchildren Islamic etiquettes of behaviour based on Quranic teachings and from the example of the prophet Muhammad. This usually involved reading relevant verses and sayings of the Prophet in Arabic and the translation in English, followed by discussions in Bengali and English. This enabled them to understand some words and stories of the Qur'ān.

Panna engaged with Aminah in activities that she prompted such as reading English books (7) she brought from school. Habib enjoyed reading his school books to Rahma as well as the books he brought from his Saturday Islamic School. Rekha tended to read more Bengali books together with Samiha. All three enjoyed telling their grandchildren stories (8) from when they were younger, and sharing *golpos and kichas* (stories and folk tales) with them. Rahma and Rekha loved telling stories about their youth and life in Bangladesh. The children liked to visit (9) their *nani's* (maternal grandmother) friends and family with them. The grandmothers all thought this was important as it allowed the children access to the older generation.

By being able to listen to the stories shared by the grandmothers' friends, the children were exposed to Bengali and the country's cultural practices. Talking about members of the family (10) was a way for the grandmothers to teach their grandchildren about the people who belonged in their extended family, especially those they had not met.

Samiha sometimes sang English nursery rhymes (11) that her grandmother liked to listen to and join in with, and she loved to sing Bengali nursery rhymes with her grandmother. Habib and his grandmother sang Arabic and English *nasheeds* (songs praising God and the prophets) together. Sometimes Aminah tried to involve *nani* in her computer games (13), showing her how to play or getting her to watch her when she was playing. When Habib played games on the computer he tried to involve Rahma but she ended up watching him most of the time. Habib watched TV and videos with his grandmother and films about Islamic history and cartoons based on Muslim heroes from the past, and Aminah and Samiha were exposed to Hindi (14) when they watched Indian Bollywood films with their grandmothers.

Aminah liked playing games (15), usually role-playing games where she took on the role of teacher or doctor and Panna was the student or patient. These role plays occupied a lot of their time together. Samiha also involved her grandmother in her role plays. Both Habib and Samiha tried to solve riddles together with their grandmothers. Riddles, folktales, proverbs, maxims, and songs are a rich tradition of Bangladeshi folklore and folk literature. It is a tradition created by the rural folk, transmitted orally from one generation to the next (Shahed, 1993). Bengali riddles are a source of pleasure for young and old alike, designed to make people inquisitive about life and the world. A riddle is usually an emotive metaphor with a question and is a manifestation of wit and intellect. A popular example is: *ek kole dui bhai – keur sathe keur dekha nai* (two brothers on the same lap, one does not meet the other – the answer is two eyes). One of the games Rekha was playing with her grandchildren during one of my visits was the traditional village game *isain bisuin* (the Bengali version of ip dip do), which the children seemed to enjoy very much.

Rahma brought Habib back and forth from school (17) quite often, as his mother worked. When the days were longer and the weather was fine, Habib liked to go to the park with her (18) on the way home from school or the mosque.

All had favourite activities they liked to do together. For Aminah and Panna it was cooking and sharing *golpos* and *kichas*. Panna used these opportunities to share fables and folk stories in Bengali, particularly as this gave her the opportunity to teach Aminah lessons in life and share information about Bangladesh and life there. Panna thought Aminah learned cultural values and manners from her and she herself learned stories and the way children lived in the UK from Aminah.

Rahma enjoyed talking to Habib about what he did at home and in school. She most liked sharing stories from the Qur'ān and Islamic books about the prophets. They shared a love for the way the prophets struggled and succeeded and how they could learn from them.

Rekha thought Samiha learned Islamic, family, and cultural values from her through the stories they shared about life in the UK and Bangladesh. She liked to teach and pass on these values to her as she felt they would help Samiha learn how to build her own Islamic character, good behaviour, and etiquette. Rekha in turn learned English from Samiha and how to greet people, for example with 'hello' and 'good morning'. Interestingly, she also mentioned that she had learned how to praise Samiha from watching her daughter Shamima and the teachers praising children. This was something new for her and sometimes difficult as it was not customary practice when she was growing up.

Although many studies have been carried out on early socialization in cross-cultural contexts, less attention has been given to the cultural context in which cognition and learning takes place, particularly within three-generation families. The initial insight into the interactions between the grandmothers and the children highlights the richness of the potential learning taking place, unique to this intergenerational relationship. It is clear that the applications of the sociocultural learning constructs of scaffolding, guided participation, synergy, and syncretism have not been fully explored within intergenerational learning in families where the grandmother, mother, and child all bring knowledge and experience (funds of knowledge) that are unique to the dynamics of their social and family interactions. Neither has prolepsis within the interactions between the grandparents and the grandchildren been given due attention by researchers or practitioners. Yet Murphy and Wolfenden (2013: 271) have revealed the 'pedagogies of mutuality' whereby teachers acknowledge children's agency and build relationships with children to enhance learning so that 'the distribution of expertise in classrooms and schools shifts and pupils and teachers become self-regulating learners'.

Part of the agency children have is the different relationships they form with adults around them and the choices they make consciously and subconsciously to develop their learner identities as they interact with these adults. The next chapter introduces the children, their mothers and grandmothers who participated in my study. I hope to give readers some insight into the dynamics of their relationships with one another and into their struggles and successes as the mothers and grandmothers settle into a host country and raise their children here in the UK.

Chapter 3
The participants

> Participation in a culture includes participation in the narratives of that culture, a general understanding of the stock of meanings and their relationships to each other.
>
> Richardson, 1990: 24

This chapter introduces the three grandmothers, Rahma, Panna, and Rekha, who share their stories, voices, struggles, and successes as they journey to a new country to better their lives and negotiate their way through building a life for themselves and their families. Three second-generation mothers share their stories of trying to integrate into British society and raise a generation of British-Bangladeshi children. These adults partly shape the stories of the three children, taking part as learners as they juggle the many jigsaw pieces of their identities to form their whole self. Interview transcripts and field notes inform the stories.

All the grandmothers came to the UK between 1970 and 1981. Their daughters would have started school in the late 1970s and mid-1980s. The grandchildren started school in the first decade of the twenty-first century. All three children attended a primary school based in the East End of London within the London Borough of Tower Hamlets. This chapter sets the current context within which intergenerational interactions are taking place in the home.

The families
Samiha's family

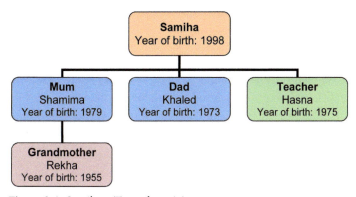

Figure 3.1: Samiha – Tree of participants

Samiha, an 8-year-old British-born Bangladeshi girl, lives in Wapping with her grandparents, uncles, aunts, first cousins, and parents, all in the same house. She has a younger sister and previously participated in Kenner *et al.*'s (2004b) study with her paternal grandparents. Now in Year 3, she participated in my study with her maternal grandmother. From the moment I was introduced to Rekha by Samiha's mother Shamima, I was referred to as *ma*, meaning mother in Bengali. This is an endearing cultural term parents use to address their daughters and I was immediately accepted as one by her. I in turn referred to her as *khala* (maternal aunt), as is an Asian custom when addressing elder women within the community.

REKHA, SAMIHA'S GRANDMOTHER
Rekha was in her early fifties, and her two sons and their families lived with her. She travelled between Bangladesh and the UK to spend time with her extended family. She arrived in the UK in the summer of 1980 at the age of 25 with two of her eldest sons, one aged 2½ years and the other just 9 months; her other four children were born in the UK. Samiha and Rekha lived within a mile of each other and saw one another every fortnight along with all of Samiha's cousins. Rekha's initial memory of the UK was shock at the way people dressed, particularly women. Culturally she was used to women covering their bodies and, as it was summer in the UK, most of the British women she first saw were wearing clothes that did not cover their arms, legs, and shoulders.

Rekha spoke mostly Bengali and a little English with her grandchildren and regarded raising her children to speak Bengali to be very important. As she said:

> ... *tarar'e tho shob shomoi amra* Bangla *mati* Bangla *jio khorsi tara* English *ghoro matise na ola oise,* English*'e tho gore mathe tahole tho amrar mathri basha tho tara buli zaibogi, amrar matri basha hoilo boro oita oilo amrar mulloban tho goro tara* Bangla *matise ba* school*'o gele tara* teacher*'er loge tara* English *tho matho oibo eta korse tara*

> ... **we always spoke** Bangla **to them and they didn't speak any** English **at home, that's how it happened, if they speak** English **at home they will forget our mother tongue, our mother tongue is very important so they spoke** Bangla **at home, but when they went to** school **they had to speak to the** teachers **in English, they did that.**

Rekha, Samiha's grandmother

All Rekha's children were fluent Bengali speakers and could read and write Bengali reasonably well, although she feared they were losing some of their reading and writing skills through lack of use and practice. Her views on her children's attitude towards teaching their children Bengali were quite clear:

> *Tara ila khorenni? Tara ila kono* Bangla *hiker ni? Tara* Bangla're *kono gurutho der ni? ...* Bangla *jene matho partho nai ekhan kono khe'al korer ni? Eta khe'al khortho oibo na khorle* Bangla *math hikbo khoi thaki?* Bangla *zodi hike na tho amar loge mathbo koi thaki ... ek shomoi jodi zai* holiday'th *tho tara tho matho farthonai, tho eta oshubida oibo*

> **Are they doing that? Are they teaching Bangla like that? Are they giving any importance to Bangla? ... They are not going to be able to speak Bangla – do they realize that? They need to realize that, otherwise where will they learn Bangla from? If they don't learn Bangla where will they learn to speak to me? ... If they go to Bangladesh they will not be able to speak and then there will be difficulties.**

Rekha

Rekha used to go into school to receive her children's reports, but found it difficult to engage with the teachers across the language barrier:

> *... gesi ansi* report *... tara ze* report'*ta dise eta phoria dekhlam kita phoraisoin bala phoraisoin na kita phoraisoin ekhano eishob buztam pharlam ne, thokhon o buzlam ar shokhol proshnor uttor disoin er laigi matham na*

> **... went and got reports ... the report they [teachers] gave read them and saw what they learned and what they didn't, and what they understood, and they answered all the questions so just didn't have to speak.**

Rekha

She explained how she supported their learning at home:

> *... onek shomoi khelsi kono shomoi khoisi tumi tain boia phoro, boi disi khata disi lekho tumi lekho othokhan hein lekho othokhan zar zei phora phoro ar lekho, ami khonotha kham khoriar* kitchen'*o bade aia tomatanor phora loimu, lekha dekhmu tara lekhse khono shomoi khorer na hurutha tho lage nai ni tho khoisi aia hokholer ath bandia thui rakhmu! ami marsi na*

... sometimes played with them, sometimes said to them you sit down and read gave them books, exercise books, said write you write and you write this much, whoever has whatever to read, read and write, I am going to work in the kitchen, after which I will come and check your reading, writing and sometimes they didn't you know kids fight with each other so I said I will tie all their hands up and leave them! But I never smacked them.

Rekha

Rekha stated her views on developing discipline:

... *kono shomoi ase ze beshi choto thakhthe zodi tare* freedom *dia dilou heshe ar* control *korta fartai na, tare kono kotha hunaitha farthai na, tare* freedom *ditai shashon o khortai mai'a o khortai tar bitrer khotha loi thai, ek shomoi khoitoi oibo na hoile tho dorai'a khoitho nai, bad'o ek jinish kore ar tumi jiggau tho tomare khoitho na i ... hokhol shomoi martai nai ekbar doibar tinbar khoi lai, hurutha buzerna ekhbar ekhshomoi marlai, marle tho emon khun nai je marle bachare mari laibo, ma'tho marbo je bad kham khorer ba bad kham khorto nai shob ma bap o tho sai nani bacha'ainthor sele hok ar me'e hok balo hoitho*

... there are times when they are too small and freedom is given then later you will not be able to control them, you cannot get them to listen to anything, give them freedom and boundaries, love them and find out what they are thinking inside, at times let them tell you, otherwise they will be too scared to say, then later they will do things and not tell you ... you shouldn't hit them all the time tell them once twice three times and the children don't understand then smack them not so much to kill them, mothers will smack to make sure children are not misbehaving all parents want whether it's a boy or a girl they should be good.

Rekha

She went on to describe how she dealt with sibling rivalry:

... *boro ze than're khoitham tumi boro bade khelaibai soto ze tare dilou he ekhon khelai'a bade tomare dibo* share *khorbo ola khorbo, tara tho* share *khora ola buse naini? amra tho khoi ze tumi boro tomare bhaia dakhtho ... bou duiuzone milaia khalou ... haradin khali mar dile oitho nai, tara tho buz mantho ar shokhol shomoi zodi khudaia khoi the mantho nai*

… say to the older one you are older you can play later give to the little one he will play with it now and will give to you later, will share with you, they understand sharing isn't it? We say you are older and he will call you *bhaia* … sit and both play together … if you smack them all day it won't work, they need to understand to reason and if you shout at them all the time they will not speak.

Rekha

When asked about how her daughter should deal with inappropriate behaviour, Rekha expressed the view that children should have some routine and that there was a manner in which children should be disciplined:

… *eta tho oilogi* time *motho khaitho, khani* time *o khe'al khortai,* school'*o gesi tesi kina khe'al khortai, eke shomoi ekhkhan khoiso hunche na martai na galithai na buzaithai, buzai'a khoithai, busbar shomoi … egu tho bustho nai* [Samiha's younger sister] *o Samiha buzbo ekhshomoi buzai'a khoile buzbo*

… they should eat on time, give attention when they are eating, check if they are going to school or not, if they don't pay heed at times don't smack and shout at them, reason with them, make them understand at the right time … this one will not understand [Samiha's younger sister] Samiha will understand if you help her to understand.

Rekha

Rekha was very concious of the fact that the mother should not be reprimanded by the grandparents in front of the children when she tries to discipline them, the child and the mother should be advised separately:

… *okhano khoi tai na ma're agla khoi tai ze 'tumi mario na buzaio', tara'reo* [the children] *khoitai 'ela khorio na amma marbai' okhta oilo boro*

… don't say it there, take the mother aside and say don't smack them help them to understand, and tell them [the children] don't do that mum will smack, that is the important thing [to explain to them].

Rekha

Samiha enjoyed role plays at home and her grandmother told me 'Ana [nickname] wants to be a doctor, she measures all our blood pressure', and Samiha contributed by saying '*ami ota nanire khori* I do this to *nani,* I touch his [grandfather's] head and see his temperature, checking pulse'. Rekha felt a part of her role was to motivate her grandchildren to achieve academically. She thought Samiha learned Islamic, family, and cultural values from her through the stories they shared about life here in the UK and in Bangladesh. She liked to teach and pass on these values to her as she felt that these would help Samiha to learn how to build her own Islamic character, good behaviour, and etiquette:

> *Ekhongu tara okhtar* [faith] *laigi taan thakhbo beshi ... okhongur* culture *oigese beshi* high *... oi mani* school'*er jio beshi taan thakhe beshi tarar huruthar etar* [faith] *baidi khom thakhbo tho etar baidi ma bafor ba shokhole eta beshi kheal khora lagbo, nizer dormo hikhaite oile ... eta tara're busite oibo khoitho oibo na khoile tho tara hiktho nai, ma'e shob kisu kora jai khe'al khorle shob kisu kora zai ... ar dada dadi ba nana nani ... khe'al khora laghbo, khe'al khorle mane tarar o balo oibo* family'*r lagi o balo oibo shob dik dia balo oibo*

> Now they will have a lot of feeling for this [faith] ... now the attraction for culture is high ... I mean if they have too much attraction for school then the children will have less feeling for this [faith] therefore mothers and fathers need to give due attention to this, if you want to teach your faith ... help them to understand, if they are not told they will not learn; mother can do everything if they pay attention to it ... and grandparents [paternal and maternal] ... need to pay attention, if attention is paid then it will be good for them, good for the family and good in every way.
>
> Rekha

Rekha would like her grandchildren to remember all the Islamic practices she tried to pass onto them:

> *... eta oilo amra tara're* Islamic *shikha dia zodi zaitam phari tara phore namaz phore,* Qur'ān *tilawat khore ar akhtha zodi amar khota mone hoi tarar dadar khota mone hoi ... namaz doi rakhat phoria ba* Qur'ān *tilwat khoria zodi tara dua khore tho okhta oilo boro*

> ... that is if I can leave Islamic teachings behind with them then they will later pray, can recite the Qur'ān and if and when they remember me or their grandad ... they will pray two lots of prayers or recite the Qur'ān and pray for us that will be great.
>
> Rekha

SHAMIMA, SAMIHA'S MOTHER

Shamima was 25 years old at the time of this study, born and raised in the UK and one of six siblings. Shamima completed her A-levels before getting married to Samiha's father, who was born in Bangladesh and came to the UK at the age of 13: 'Oh he loves Bangladesh he has to go once or twice a year ... so he is very attached to Bangladesh.' She was a full-time mother to two daughters, Samiha and Surayah. Shamima visited Bangladesh twice but she only remembered the second time she went at the age of 10:

> It was wonderful and I didn't want to come back, everything was different the weather, the atmosphere, it was so green, colourful ... it was just fun and exciting, my granddad, my uncles were there and it was just lovely ... I wish I was born in Bangladesh ... cuz it was just like so much freedom and the culture it was just completely different from this country.
>
> Shamima, Samiha's mother

Shamima remembered her earliest memories of raising her daughter in the UK as being wonderful and quite a family experience, as Samiha was the first daughter/granddaughter in the extended family. Up to the age of 3 Samiha spent a lot of time with her grandparents, 'just going places or in the garden she would want to go out every time ... so her grandma or granddad just used to walk about around the canal or they used to sit in the garden and make her water the plants just so she could stay outside [laughing]'. Both her daughters were spoken to in Bengali and English at home, 'eh when they were younger I spoke a lot of Bangla but now they've picked up on English and stuff and you tend to talk English with them, they talk Bangla with their grandparents coz they talk to them in that language' and the sisters speak to each other in Bengali as the younger one tends to only speak in Bengali.

Shamima had hopes for her daughters to be highly educated, and was pleased that the school supported the children in achieving their potential. Parents were kept well informed of what was being covered in school so that they could support their children at home. Shamima was also a parent governor at the school: '... they always include the parents in a lot of things, they have a lot of training courses, parents English classes that goes on in schools so they work around the community'. Shamima had a positive and long-standing relationship with the teachers, as other members of her family had previously attended the school. In her own education, her mother played more of an active role than her father:

80 and 20 ... ahhm more involved was my mum coz at that time
dad had to work a lot, so when he did have the time he used to
sit and spend time with us and we used to act as news reporters
and ... we also used to do a lot of like word search and stuff,
and my mum she picked up all the English language as well from
us basically, and at that time there wasn't any language classes
around for parents to learn so mum played a more active role
when I think about it.

Shamima

Although she was more involved in the children's life at school, her husband
was more informed about their children's education than her father was:

... err I don't know 60 and 40? [laughing] 60 me! ... it's natural
coz the mother is always at home so if I was a working mother
that could have been different, it could have been father more
and 50/50 but I play an active role but you know there's also the
grandparents as well coz they're always there.

Shamima

Shamima was also pleased that the teachers recognized Samiha's
grandparents, as they sometimes take her to school and pick her up at the
end of the day. She felt that there was a community spirit, 'so everybody
recognizes everyone all the parents know whose child is whose so it's a well-
known area the whole community knows everybody well'.

Shamima wanted to pass on the same values she was given by her
parents, of being respectful to elders, having a consistently positive way of
thinking, empathizing with others and trying to make others happy as well
as herself. However, there were differences in the way she dealt with sibling
rivalry, 'she [Rekha] would sort of not shout or hit us or anything like that
... I get mad more often ... yeah she never used to get angry so quickly but I
do'. She also felt they learned differently with their grandmother:

... she's more relaxed with them, they feel more comfortable
asking about things and doing whatever ... whereas if Samiha
was to ask me something then she thinks I will say no or 'it's not
the time now' or this or that ... oh she learns a lot more with my
mum ... she's wonderful with them, she loves them they love her
and they are naughty, and when I'm telling them off she will be
telling me off, and she will be like 'stop telling them off all the
time there's certain ways of telling them and they will listen'. And
you think oh they never do but then she will point out that, 'if

you say it like this it would have, and then you think well she's right but we just tend to do things quickly and not even think about it ... ehm oh they learn lots of folk songs [laughs] from Bangladesh. I mean she'd be playing funny games with them they'll be laughing they will be coming to tell you oh you know *nani* said this *nani* said that can we do this can we do that ... you think oh I haven't got the time, go and do it with your *nani*. She'll be like *nani*'s not here she said to do it with you when you come home ... yes it is, it is really valuable ... sometimes you think oh go and stay at your *nani*'s house and stay there forever!

Shamima

Shamima noticed the differences between the context in which she was raising her children and that in which her mother raised her:

> ... it's really different because ehm eh I have my in-laws and I live with my in-laws so there's a certain support whereas we used to live with just my mum and dad and we didn't have our grandparents, [they] were back home so ehm it was different it's just mum at home and dad at work.

Shamima

One of the reasons for this difference was the lack of other relatives in the UK who lived nearby. Particularly when older relatives or friends visited, Shamima tried to talk to them about how her children should behave and felt she couldn't have the same expectations of her daughters as her mother had of her and her siblings: 'No it's just that I would think they're still little and they can just learn slowly as they grow up. They tend to be more spoilt now the children, even when they would become teenagers, I could but I doubt that they will [Shamima laughs].' Shamima felt there were certain expectations from her as a child:

> ... yeah we had more of a role to play ... really be good and salaam [Arabic greeting] and respect all that was due and ehm ... salaaming yeah I'm remembering all those things when I was a teenager so there was always 'Shamima put the kettle on' so make tea and *nasta* [snacks] for the people and greet them politely and we chat and leave them to enjoy their tea.

Shamima

Shamima stressed that it was because of the family Samiha had around her that she was very sociable: '... she will get to know you in a minute and will be talking about her own life story to you and finding out everything about you [laughs], so she is really good with communicating with people a lot'. However, living with extended family had its own difficulties; she felt she wasn't able to give them as much individual attention as she wanted because she had to accommodate others and give in to what was happening in the house:

> I let her watch more TV than usual coz she will moan oh other brother is watching why can't I and you just have to sometimes give in to her yeah but if it was just me on my own maybe I don't think she would have that chance to say, oh he's watching it or she's watching it, can I watch it.
>
> Shamima

She had fond memories of her grandparents when they came to stay with them in the UK for a couple of years. They had a good relationship and were close: 'Yes always getting attention and whatever we wanted we always got all we had to do was call our grandad [laughs].' Shamima also had a wonderful relationship with her parents: 'I can't remember my parents ever telling me off or anything it was just normal, perfect and nice.'

Shamima wanted her children to remember her parents as 'lovable *nanas* and *nanis* you know, always there for them they wished they were always there for them forever [laughs]'. In her own case, she wanted them to remember her as 'like how I am [laughs] ... normal happy mum and you know a mum who is always there for them someone they can always rely on'.

Aminah's family

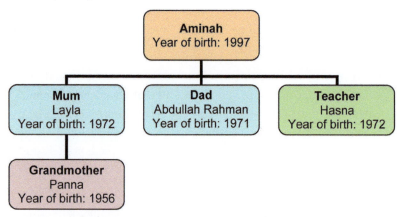

Figure 3.2: Aminah – Tree of participants

Aminah and Samiha were in the same class in Year 3 at Dockside School, which made them an interesting pair to follow, as they had the same class teacher. Aminah, an 8-year-old British-born Bangladeshi girl did not live in the borough and was brought to school every day by one of her parents. She lived within a mile of her paternal grandparents and within ten miles of her maternal grandmother.

PANNA, AMINAH'S GRANDMOTHER

Panna came to the UK to join her husband in 1972 as a new bride. She was 16 and expecting their first child. Her initial memory of coming to the UK was the deep feelings of loss, as she had to leave all her family and come to a new land. Their first residence was a flat in Brick Lane in the London Borough of Tower Hamlets, where she felt lonely and experienced the night-and-day difference to living in a village that was open and lively. Panna's husband owned a garment factory, which meant that a lot of the childcare and household responsibilities fell on her. The couple had four children who were quite close in age, with Aminah's mother, Layla, being the eldest. When the children were still quite young, the family moved to a house with a garden in Hackney, a neighbouring borough. All their four children are now married and Panna has eight grandchildren, Layla's three children being the eldest. Her youngest son and his family lived with her and her other grandchildren came to visit her once or twice a week. In 1998, at the age of 42, Panna lost her husband.

Panna's wish was to raise her children just as she would have done if she were living in Bangladesh. So she tried to preserve some of the Bangladeshi cultural and faith values by augmenting the children's normal routine of doing what was required in the UK, going to school and doing their homework. She would teach them Bengali at home and take them to Qur'ān classes during the weekends. Panna took her role as a mother seriously by teaching her children herself, as there was no network of support available. She took every opportunity to teach them:

Gore jokhon silo khela dula korto ba boshle Arabic *jototuku pari ba* Bangla *jototuku eirokom arki ... adob kaida, uta bosha, mara mari na kore ei doroner ar ki*

When they were at home they used to play and when they used to sit I taught them whatever Arabic I could or Bangla I could ... morals and manners, how to sit and walk, not to fight, things like that.

Panna, Aminah's grandmother

Panna did not attend classes to learn English, but she took it upon herself to learn as much as she could from conversing with the teachers, neighbours, and on her visits to the doctors. Although she tended to speak to her grandchildren in both Bengali and English as is shown in Table 2.1, she raised her own children speaking mostly in Bengali. Panna was proud of the fact that they all could still read and write Bengali but was not happy that Layla didn't use it due to '*beshi* time *nai* **not have much** time'.

Panna also put emphasis on teaching the cultural and religious values and practices to her children, and she felt she needed to pass them on to her grandchildren as well. This can also be seen in Table 2.1, which records that she read the Qur'ān in Arabic with Aminah and they learned about Islam together from stories in the Qur'ān through translations and Islamic books.

Panna never saw her grandfather but has fond memories of him and had vivid memories of her maternal grandmother, who passed away in 1972, the year of Panna's marriage. Panna used to spend a lot of time with her grandmother as she used to visit her often with her own mother: '*Shob shomoi nanir shathe thaktam, rathre tho shudu golpo ar golpo* **Used to stay with** *nani* [maternal grandmother] **all the time, and at night there were stories after stories.**' She reflected on her own relationship with her *nani* being very different to the one with her own grandchildren. Panna expressed this eloquently:

> ... *deshe ar aideshe, onek kiso* different. *Ai deshe* different *basha, oder shather je nathi nathinder shather* culture *milaie chola, oder basha o jana lage ar amader tho ki chilo? Amra amader nanir shathe shob shomoi cholsi amra shob shomoi buztam ora tho shob shomoi buze na, tho buzaite hoi tader basha dia* English *dia*

> ... **there is a lot of** difference **between here and there. Here there is a** different **language, to understand and get along with their culture you need to know their language, and what did we have? We stayed and got along with our** *nani* **all the time and understood them, they** [her own grandchildren] **don't always understand and you need to do that with their language** English.

Panna

Panna had little contact with the school. She used to rely on the teachers to contact her if there were any problems:

> ... *amar bachader kono* complain *ashe nai* ... complain *ashe nai je ora* homework *kore nai ba eita kore nai erokom kono kiso hoi nai* ... *shob shomoi* excellent *prai shomoi bolto je ora balo kortese*

... I never received any complaints about my children ... no complaints that they did not do their homework, nothing like that happened ... always excellent most of the time they [teachers] used to say that they [children] are doing well.

Panna

When the children brought their school reports home she used to respond postively. However she always expected positive reports as she had good discipline at home:

> *Oder shob shomai eta khe'al thakto je* homework *ta shesh kore er phore* TV *ta dekhto ... hath muk doie cha* biscuit *ba* toast *ja khai khea nilo, er pore dosh* minute *dekhenilo ba* half an hour *ektu rest nau tar pore abar* homework *kore nau, abar* right away *jodi poraite boshi ta hole porbe na thokhon kiso* freedom *doa lage*

They were always aware that they needed to complete homework before watching TV ... after washing hands and face they had tea and biscuits or toasts, after which watch ten minutes or half an hour of rest then it's homework again, again if I ask them to sit right away to study then they will not so you need to give them a little freedom.

Panna

Panna advised Layla to do the same with her children:

> *... ami koi oderke boli o kaj korte saise na ekhon onno ta korok, ei rokom korio na beshi shashon kora balo na, beshi shashon korle noshto hoie zai kono kono shomoi boli oke ... shob shomoi boli na maje modhe boli jokhon boli abar oder shamne boli na shamne bolle tho abar oshubida, alada boli ... boli eirokom hobena tumi rag korle bujaia bolbe eita korba na eita korba*

... I say I tell them that they [child] do not want to do that now, let them do something else, don't do that with them [children], too much discipline is not good, if you discipline them too much they will become bad, I tell them sometimes ... don't tell them always only sometimes and when I do I don't do it in front of them [children] as there are problems with that, tell them separately ... say it will not work like that when you [mother] are upset explain to them [children] don't do this do this.

Panna

When the children used to argue Panna found it easy to simply distract them:

Jogra korle tho shoraia nitham, ekhtake shoraia boltam je na tumi ekhon ekhane thako na o naughty hoie ... amar ekta obbash silo bachara mara mari korle oitake niea onno dike khelar dike ba ami eita dimu oita dimo oirokom kore shoraia ditam

When they used to argue I used to move them apart and say no you stay here, they are naughty ... I had a habit when the children used to fight I used to distract them to something else [by saying] I will give you this and that and move them away from each other.

Panna

Panna did not think Aminah's teachers were aware of the fact that she was Aminah's grandmother, or of what they did together, as she did not visit the school at all due to ill health and distance. However, she did think Aminah talked about her in school: '... *jani na o alap kore kina nishchoi kore* **don't know if she discusses me I'm sure she does.'**

When asked how she would like her grandchildren to remember her, Panna responded:

Eita ar ki bolar ase tilwat korbe, ba namaz porbe ba dua darood porbe eita amar me'er kase ase tara nishchoi korbe asha kori

What else can be said they will recite, pray [obligatory prayers] **and pray** [for goodness] **my daughter has that and they will surely do it I hope.**

Panna

And her hopes for her grandchildren were that '*bachara jeno balo bhabe cholbe balo bhabe shikhe* Arabic'ta, Bangla, *ma bapke jeno srodha kore boroder shonman kora, soto bhai bonder maia mohoboth kora eita ar ki* **the children are well behaved and learn Arabic, Bangla, respect their parents and honour their elders, love their younger brothers and sisters and that's it.'**

LAYLA, AMINAH'S MOTHER

Born in London to first-generation Bangladeshi British parents, Layla lived with her own three children and husband in Redbridge, a neighbouring borough of Tower Hamlets. She was 33 years old and was working full time. Layla's husband was born in Bangladesh and came to the UK with his parents when he was 5 years old. He also worked full time and was involved in his local community.

Layla and her husband became parents at the age of 18 and 19 respectively, and she reflected on her own journey as a young parent:

> I think it was a struggle in the sense we had Tahira and we were a bit kinda lost, because we were trying to understand Islam more and ehm and not more about the culture side, and cultural values. We didn't really look into that because we were normal western children. We've had a child, we were very young 19 and 18 and we were more engulfed in the general just bringing up, we weren't too much fixated on what culture says or what Islam says. But after a certain time then we decided to go into Islam and I was always doing my Islamic duties. And I think he [husband] was finding his feet in that, and then he became very I think he was more intrigued in Islam than me, that's how Islam came into play, by the time Aminah came along Islam became the most significant, it wasn't even about culture.
>
> Layla, Aminah's mother

Layla's father passed away when she was 24, and she had to shoulder many of the family responsibilities at a young age. This had an impact on the relationship between Layla and her mother:

> I think my relationship with my mum was a very intriguing one in the fact that she was there but I wouldn't get too close to her because I know that she's not very well and won't be around for long so it was like ... then it would be less heart breaking, you know so with my mum for the last 25 years or so she was really not well so I would always call her and say 'what you doing?', I wouldn't go and visit her much, coz obviously sister-in-laws are there to help and stuff like that and my brothers are always there ... I don't think we had a good relationship to the way I have with my kids in the fact that I don't think I'm a good parent. No-one's a good parent coz everyone's always explores in what is a good parent to be, but how are you meant to be a good parent? You always learn and then you're always trying to pass the wisdom onto other people you know. This is how you should do it.
>
> Layla

Layla felt that her parents had a traditional and hands-off approach to parenting and didn't take much interest in her academic performance, particularly at school. This was in contrast to her mother expressing her view that she did not need to interact with the school as Layla was well behaved and concerns were not raised, which meant that any further interaction with school was not required. All Layla's academic achievements were after marriage.

Layla's experience of the parent–teacher relationship was different to her mother's. She was very keen to see her children achieve and was thus driven to have a positive relationship with the teachers and made an extra effort to go and speak to them about her children's progress: 'I have spoken to them several occasions because I feel that they need to know who I am, they need to know who my children are so they know where they have to develop their learning needs.' She not only read their reports but also felt it was very important to go through them with the children and look at ways they could set targets and identify their needs, as well as the type of support she and the teachers could provide.

Layla's aspirations for her children were high, but she wanted them to be in touch with those around them and to include a mixture of individual aspiration and community participation:

> I want them to go and get a job, I think more community-based coz I think I've got that streak of helping people. I would like them (her children) to go into that ... I want them to be good Muslim young people, ehm I want them to be good educators to help people.
>
> Layla

Although Layla's own relationship with her mother was different in nature, she was dependent on her mother's advice and support both emotionally and practically with raising her own children. Particularly when they were younger, her mother played a key role as Layla was a youth worker in the evenings:

> ... my mum loved my kids ... My mum was a part of their lives when they were growing up ... ehm Aminah tended to spend a lot of her time with my mum generally ... so I used to go and drop her off and go straight to work, and then pick her up afterwards so she [grandmother] would be babysitting for three hours or so.
>
> Layla

As Layla's mother's illness increased, it limited her ability to take on the childcare duties for her grandchildren. Consequently, Layla relied on the local community centre where the workers were very supportive. The centre also had a Qur'ān class that the children attended.

Layla remembered speaking Bengali to her parents when she was a young mother, as was expected from her, but she raised her own children speaking only English: 'I'll try to speak Bengali sometimes but it just doesn't kind of fit in.' She explained proudly her children's interest in languages:

Tahira can speak Spanish, French, English and little Bangla ... very little but she understands Bangla very well and she can also understand Arabic as well, Iqbal can speak Arabic and understands you know he can communicate in Arabic and English ... Aminah, she tries Bangla sentences it's so strange she's probably the only one who tries the Bangla.

Layla

Layla attributed this interest in learning Bengali to the time Aminah, her daughter, spent with her grandmother. She did give her parents credit for her own competence as a bilingual, as it was due to their diligence in speaking Bengali with her and her siblings that they spoke Bengali competently.

Aminah also learned from her grandmother the value of being helpful and caring towards others. Layla stressed that the relationship the children had with their grandmother was very different to her own:

... yeah because they have different learning and teaching ehm methods, I mean its just being around, they [children] learn so many things, kind of has a presence you know it's just like you know how to ... playing games you know I would do it differently. I would say there are rules you need to follow and their [grandmother] like, we just play snakes and ladders you know they're more relaxed, let's have fun and enjoy that kind of arena, whereas I'm sitting there saying we have to follow the rules ... uhm yeah when we did used to visit, she [grandmother] will just relax and there was this, oh shall I make this or shall I make that and the kids are around, but with me, I mean just generally speaking about mothers I think we're more of the controlling sort.

Layla

Layla hoped her children would remember her as a loving mother:

Whatever I did was best for them and they need to make lots of *dua* [prayers] for me, and they have to remember me as not as a figure, but they need to remember the qualities I had was for a reason and what I was trying to do was best for them. So they need to say ok maybe mum was right when they bring up their own kids.

Layla

Her desire was for them to remember their grandparents as 'how they are, *nani* was there she loved them, she cared for them'.

Habib's family

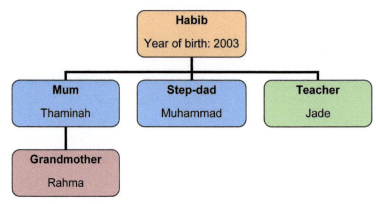

Figure 3.3: Habib – Tree of participants

Habib is a 6-year-old British-born Bangladeshi boy in Year 2 at Dockside School. He is the eldest child of three. His mother, Thaminah, is a primary school teacher and his grandmother, Rahma, takes on a lot of the childcare duties when his mum is at work.

RAHMA, HABIB'S GRANDMOTHER

Rahma came to the UK at Christmas in 1977 when she was aged 25. She left all her family and friends behind to join her husband, who had lived in the UK since he was a young child. She laughed when she remembered her memories of arriving at the airport:

> *Mone ase ya* Allah *ek bare andar!* Christmas'*e ashsilam, snow khita silo gho* airport'*e eshe dekhi* snow *ekbare kono gaas'e patha nai thea ami kotho shomoi phore boli 'ei desher patha ki zou kisu khae nise?'*

> **I remember yes** Allah **it was totally dark! Came during** Christmas, **oh there was not just** snow, **when I came to the** airport **I just saw** snow **and there were absolutely no leaves on the trees, after a while I asked 'did something eat all the leaves of this country?'**

Rahma, Habib's grandmother

She reminisced about her reaction to the house she was to live in:

> ... *furana ghore silam ami ghor dekhi ami bolsilam 'na ami ei deshe thakhbona ei deshe kono gusul korar bebosta nai ami thakbo na ami sole zabo', tho uni bole 'tumi ki rokom zaba?' 'Tho* Bethnal Green *dia tho* bus *zai ami bolsi oi* bus'*e ute sole zabo'*

> ... **stayed in an old house, after I saw the house, I said 'I don't want to stay in this country, there aren't any facilities to have a wash I will not stay I want to go', so he [husband] said 'how will you go?' So I said 'the bus that goes through Bethnal Green I will get on that and go'.**

Rahma

Rahma had lost two sons at birth before she came to the UK. She went on to have two daughters and two sons, of whom Thaminah was the eldest. She lost another son at birth about 15 months after Thaminah's birth: '*[J]odi* Bangladesh'*e zaitam phartam tahole ektu balo hoitho amar jonno* [laughs] *ami* help *paitam shobai* help *kortho ... eka eka feel kortam na* **[I]f I could go to Bangladesh then it would have been good for me** [laughs], **I would have got help everyone would have helped ... would not feel all alone.'** She spent a lot of time at home with the children when they were younger as they were all close in age.

Rahma never managed to work, although the teachers at her children's school could see her potential and bilingual skills and wanted her to become a teaching assistant:

> ... teacher *der shathe balo shomporko silo alap khortho, khotha boltho, saitho ze 'tumi kaz koro kaz korle amader* school'*e sele meader onek laab hobe, tumi* Bangla *bashai zodi khotha bolo onek laab hobe' kintu shomoi pai nai*

> ... **I had a good relationship with the** teachers, **they used to discuss things, talk and said that 'you should work, if you work it will really benefit the girls and boys in our** school, **if you speak in** Bangla **language it will really help' but I didn't have time.**

Rahma

The teachers' enthusiasm could have been due to the deputy head of the school being himself bilingual and very interested in bilingualism.

As Rahma's husband did not speak much Bengali, she felt it was her duty to maintain their language while the children were growing up:

> ... *ami icha kore bolthan ami zodi* English *boli ami shikhbo kintu oderke jodi* Bangla *shikhaithe pari thaole tho lab hobe ami mone khortam ze* English *tho shikboi shikbo ur baba tho* English *ekhon tho* Bangla *boltei pare na!*

> ... I purposefully spoke, if I speak English I will learn but if I can teach them Bangla it will be beneficial, I used to think that they will definitely learn English, their dad is English and he can't speak Bangla at all!

Rahma

She said Thaminah did not speak Bengali to her children:

> ... *she* Bangla *ta bole na* [laughs] *bole 'ze amma amar jodi* Bangla *bolte hoi tho amar onek shomoi lage oder shathe kotha bolte er jonno ami* English'*e bole ni'*

> ... she doesn't speak Bangla [laughs] says 'see *amma* [mum] if I have to speak Bangla it takes me a long time to speak to them that's why I just say it in English'.

Rahma

About her grandchildren she said '*na ora tho shudhu amar shathe* Bangla *bole ar karo shathe* Bangla *bole na oder abbu'r shathe'o bole na* no they only speak Bangla with me and with no-one else not even their daddy'. Her passion was to raise her children with high moral values and give them a good education.

As her relationship with her grandchildren was close, Rahma felt she was able to advise Thaminah on how she should behave with them:

> ... *poramorsho dei ze Thaminah ethotuku koris na etho soto soto bacha bolbe ze 'eder zalai kichu korte pari na!' thokhon amar dukho lage, ei duzon tho ekkebare soto*

> ... I advise her don't do so much [discipline]! Such small small children she says 'I can't do anything because of their pestering!' Then I feel sad, these two are very little.

Rahma

But she felt they behaved well when they were with her:

> *Oderke boi gula dekhai boli ze* Arabi *pora'ta poro tho she pore ar boli tomar ma ashle ar bolthe hobe na ze poro ar* English'*er kotha bola o lage na boshle ektar por ekta boi ane ar pore*

I show them the books and say read the Arabic and they do, and
I say when your mummy comes she won't have to tell you to read,
and with the English books I don't have to tell them when they sit
they get one after the other and read.

Rahma

Rahma felt that although the teachers knew her – as they often saw her
picking Habib up and dropping him off – they never showed interest in
speaking to her: '… teacher *der shathe beshi mila misha kori na ami bahir're
thekhe nia ashi ar zei din* programme *hoi* Thaminah *zai ba amra doi zon'ei
zai mile mishe* I don't speak to the teachers much just pick them up from
outside and when there is a programme on, Thaminah and I go together.'
However, she had a good relationship with the mothers who went to pick
up their children and they knew her well.

Rahma's paternal grandparents passed away, leaving her father
orphaned at a young age. Her paternal grandfather came from Afghanistan
to Bangladesh and married her grandmother. She had few memories of
her maternal grandfather, but fondly remembered spending time with her
grandmother eating lots of wonderful food, being bathed, and also sharing
lots of stories. People from the village would also share stories of her
paternal grandparents, which she enjoyed listening to. She herself spent a
lot of time with her three young grandchildren, often spending days with
them at their home.

When asked what she would like to leave behind for her grandchildren
she said:

> … *ar ki dibo? amar tho ar taka poisha ruzi kori nai taka poisha
> tho dite parbo na, ekzon balo manush hoa'r jonno je jinish ta
> dorkar* Allah'*ke bhoi paoa, er pore manush'er shathe mile mishe
> chola phira, ora tho khortese ami tho dekhtesi*

… what else can I give? I don't earn money so I can't give that, to
be a good person what they need is to fear Allah, and then to be
able to live with others well, they are doing these I can see.

Rahma

Rahma desired that Habib prays for her when she passes away:

> Habib'*ke Madrashai disi etai tho asha kori ze eta zodi shike tho
> amar zonno she dua korbe ar shobar saithe tho mone ki amar
> jonno dua korbe … Amar kotha etai mone rakhbe ze amar nanu
> ekhane boshe* Qur'ān *portho tho amake antho*

Mahera Ruby

Habib goes to madrasa so the hope is he will learn from it and pray, and pray for me the most ... he should remember about me that his *nanu* used to sit here [mosque] and read Qur'ān and used to bring me [from school].

Rahma

THAMINAH, HABIB'S MOTHER

Thaminah was 30 years old. She was born in London and lived with her husband and children who were all born in the East End of London. Thaminah went to Dockside School (the same primary school as her children) and memories and stories told by her mother about her and her siblings suggested she was regarded as the child who was quiet and shy. She remembered learning to read soon after going to school and the support received from her younger brother and mum helped Thaminah immensely. It had been a difficult journey to begin with. Thaminah recalled her lack of confidence in sport activities:

So my mum used to morally support me at sports days, and even sitting with me during swimming lessons until I learned how to swim. It was embarrassing that I was the only child who had my mum having to sit with me, but my teachers were supportive and encouraged mum's involvement.

Thaminah, Habib's mother

Thaminah also remembered receiving support from her mum with maths. Her mother attended extra numeracy sessions and took part in extracurricular activities as part of the family learning classes that took place at the school.

Habib's biological father lived in London and spent a couple of hours with him every two weeks. When Habib was 4 years old, Thamima remarried and had two other children:

Habib has a wonderful relationship with my husband [step-father], and I really believe that this was established prior to our marriage as he built up a relationship with him during that time. Their relationship now is truly like father and son and I see no difference between how Habib and his younger siblings are treated.

Thaminah

Her early experiences of bringing up Habib were quite painful, as circumstances were difficult. She distracted herself by utilizing the local park, providing Habib with an enriching experience: 'As an educator I believe that parents can support the child's experiences, and broaden their life experiences by introducing elements into their lives early on and I have truly tried my best to support this ethos.'

Thaminah said she had a warm and loving relationship with her mother: 'I can tell my mother everything in my life and I know she will listen and advise me accordingly.' Her mother was part of their everyday lives, as she spent most of her time with them. The children kept her occupied and were good company for her, since she was unwell most of the time.

When Habib was born, he was spoken to in Bengali, the language spoken at home. His grandmother had a tremendous influence on him, as he spent a great deal of time with her. Thaminah returned to studying when Habib was a year old. Her mother raised Habib and later settled him into school, taking him there and back. Habib spoke Bengali well: 'The bond between them is very strong, loving, affectionate, comfortable and trusting, often he wasn't confident to speak to me regarding a matter but he would speak to my mum about the situation to ease his feelings.' Habib now spoke Bengali to his grandmother, as this was what he felt comfortable using, English with his father, and a mixture of both languages with his siblings. They did many activities at home and in the community together. When Habib was younger, he used to enjoy role play situations, being a fireman, builder, train driver, mechanic, chef, etc. He also enjoyed 'playing in the park, taking an adventure pack with him to go hunting or mountaineering. He enjoys being outdoors and we use the warmer weather to support his love of the great outdoors.' Habib also developed a fondness for gardening, which he shared with his grandparents, who had their own allotment plot where they grew many vegetables throughout the year. Habib went there often with them.

Thaminah's parents' relationship with her teachers was similar to her own with Habib's teachers. They were able to approach the teachers without any difficulties or give support from home when needed. Her mum played an active role during their primary years; she always took them to school and took care of their needs during the formative years of their childhood. When they went to secondary school, their father attended parents' evenings as he had a better command of English. Thaminah's relationship with Habib's teachers had always been positive: 'I have been able to speak to his teachers regarding matters as and when it was needed. It has become known to his teachers that I was working in schools myself and this has given him a somewhat greater expectation to do better than his peers.' Her aspirations for all her children were the same and much like those of the other two mothers: she wanted the children 'to progress as individuals, to have faith and to make it a real life experience, to have self-discipline, to have courage, to know what is right and wrong, to acquire good morals and manners and be a good citizen in society'.

Habib's relationship with his grandmother differed from the one he had with Thaminah:

> My mum has a very easy-going approach to allowing children to try their own way first and then allow them to be directed when they come to a difficult hurdle. My mum had this attitude with us as children and she has allowed Habib to do the same, by feeling at ease with her and not being directive he can turn to her for support at any time.
>
> Thaminah

Interestingly, all three mothers shared a similar feeling about the way their own mothers were more relaxed and approachable with their grandchildren than with them.

Both sets of grandparents lived in Bangladesh, and Thaminah's mother took them to see their grandparents once when they were young children. They didn't spend long with their paternal grandparents; most of their two-month visit was spent with their maternal grandmother:

> She came with us on all our visits to countless aunts' and uncles' houses. I have a fond memory of our time that I spent with my maternal grandmother. It was a very enriching experience building a strong relationship of love and kindness and enjoying her.
>
> Thaminah

Thaminah would like her children to remember her parents fondly for all the good things they did together. She hoped they would share these memories with their own children and impart to them the moral values held by the grandparents, 'the happiness and joy that we share as a family'. She hoped that they would take on the values of discipline, be confident to try new things, and take part in extracurricular activities that would support them as individuals. Habib enjoyed much more support from Thaminah's mother than his siblings did; he was the first grandchild and spent a considerable amount of time with her during his formative years. When asked how she would like the children to remember her, Thaminah replied hesitantly:

> This is rather a difficult question to answer, erm, I hope to instil in them a sense of love, which they will pass on to their own

children, that their earliest memories are that they were cherished and loved and that I did my utmost to be there for them. I provided for them throughout their lives and we had a good time through all the difficulties, the fact that I didn't give up when it was tough.

Thaminah

From these conversations it can be seen that the three grandmothers shared the daunting experience of being a mother in an unfamiliar country. They had to endure their sense of loneliness and isolation not only as individuals but also as mothers. The grandmothers' own education was not extensive: before their marriages, Panna had only completed her primary education, and Rekha and Rahma their high school education. Their attitude towards their own children's schooling were the same; all had faith that the schools were doing their best for their children. However, they were all vigilant in maintaining their children's Bengali, faith practices and cultural values. This was difficult for all of them, as there were few community classes or tutors, so they had to rely on their own learning and experiences. The grandmothers also shared similar thoughts and feelings about the values they wished to pass on to their grandchildren, which were predominantly around maintaining Bengali as well as their faith and cultural values and practices. The grandmothers had in common the unique experience of becoming grandparents and the particular joy of watching their children parenting the next generation and witnessing the continuation of the family lineage.

The three second-generation mothers enjoyed the support of their parents in their personal growth as well as when raising their own children. All three mothers had a lot more interaction with their children's school and teachers than their own parents had had. What was common between the mothers and grandmothers was the interest in teaching the children their faith values and both generations' recognition of the role the grandmothers played in maintaining their Bengali language.

The next chapter explores the intergenerational interactions between Aminah, Samiha, and Habib with their teachers, Jade and Hasna.

Chapter 4

Exploring intergenerational learning between children and their teachers

This chapter begins with a look at the research studies to date that capture the way children learn at school. It highlights that scaffolding is still a key construct used within classrooms to support children's learning. I then introduce the teachers, their views on teaching and learning and their thoughts on Aminah, Samiha, and Habib as learners in their classrooms. Using segments of the transcripts from the jigsaw puzzle interactions, I describe turn-taking and question-and-answer patterns to highlight the role of each activity in aiding learning.

Children's learning at school

> As the school was hierarchical in nature, I needed to maintain the channel of authority. My initial contact was with the head teacher, to seek his permission to carry out my personal research in his school. I was asked to send him a proposal and an indication of what I expected from the teachers and the timescale of my involvement with the teachers. With my partial insider awareness of the internal politics of the school, I had to accept that the power of the head teacher would enable me to gain access to the teachers, whom I knew well. Such insider knowledge enabled me to set up a meeting with Hasna and Jade, the two class teachers of the participant children, to see the best way forward. I entered the research arena believing that I had, through my privileged access to the participants and our shared experience of the previous project, the opportunity to explore my role within their classrooms and the collection of data.
>
> Fieldnotes, 2006

Hasna was the class teacher for the Year 4 class where Samiha and Aminah were students. Jade was the class teacher for Habib. In the first months I spent at least a couple of sessions a week in their classrooms, getting to know their ways of teaching and their interactions with the children (see my fieldnotes above). As Luke and Kale (1997) observe, children bring to school knowledge that is drawn from their interactions in their lives outside of school:

> The differences that children bring to classrooms are not simply individual differences or idiosyncrasies. They are the products and constructions of the complex and diverse social learning from the cultures where children grow, live and interact ... these, too, are dynamic and hybrid: mixing, matching and blending traditional values and beliefs, child-rearing practices and literacy events with those of new, post-modern popular cultures.
>
> Luke and Kale, 1997: 13

Teachers often use the learning construct of scaffolding to describe how they develop children as learners. Holton and Clarke (2006: 131) defined scaffolding as 'an act of teaching that (i) supports the immediate construction of knowledge by the learner; and (ii) provides the basis for future independent learning of an individual'. This idea of the expert supporting the novice to move to the next stage is defined by Vygotsky (1978) as the Zone of Proximal Development (ZPD), which is

> ... the distance between the actual developmental level as determined by independent problem solving and the level of potential development as determined through problem solving under adult guidance or in collaboration with more capable peers.
>
> Berk and Winsler, 1995: 76

Vygotsky maintained that it is helpful to assess children's abilities to solve a problem through the process of an expert assisting a novice learner or apprentice. The teacher as the expert becomes responsible for children's cognitive development as they work with them in their ZPD. Crucial to a sociocultural approach, where young children learn as apprentices alongside a more experienced member of the culture, is the role of the mediator. According to Gregory *et al.* (2004: 7), the mediator is 'the teacher, adult or more knowledgeable sibling or peer' who initiates 'children into new cultural practices or guide[s] them in the learning of new skills'.

Wells (1986) observed the role of instruction, the nature of talk, and the nature of questioning during an interaction between children and teachers. He found that the pattern of interaction was different at home and at school: children spoke more at home than at school, where they tended to ask fewer questions and had fewer chances to speak. The meanings children expressed at home and at school were different, too: at school, they tended to use syntactically simpler sentences and express a smaller range of meanings. This, Wells argued, was because teachers did most of the talking in the classroom, determining the topic of the talk and initiating most of the questions and requests.

In addition to the lack of response time for the pupils, the social interaction patterns used in the classroom could well be different to those in the home cultures. Tharp (1994) documented cultural differences in how language is used in educational settings – for example, how stories are told, the ways in which teachers give response time to students during questioning sequences, the rhythmic patterns of the verbal interactions, and the patterns of conversational turn-taking. The turn-taking patterns in interactions between the children and the adults during their puzzle activities were hugely significant.

Hasna, Aminah and Samiha's teacher

Hasna was Aminah and Samiha's class teacher. She is a 29-year-old British-Bangladeshi Sociology graduate. Born in Bangladesh, she arrived in the UK at the age of 3. After graduating, Hasna spent a year working as a teaching assistant. Although she had had no intention of going into teaching before, her work as an assistant inspired her to complete a Post Graduate Certificate in Education (PGCE). When the present study was conducted, she had been teaching for seven years and the practical knowledge and practice during her training prepared her for teaching in inner-city schools, as her lecturers had been culturally aware: 'Some of the activities we did we would do as groups and then we'd share practices and we would go off and do it ourselves so some of the activities I still use, they were really useful.' Hasna went on to complete her PGCE research project on the topic of whether or not children's books reflected their cultures, as she felt a lot of books didn't do so at the time.

Hasna's bilingual and bi-literate skills were gained through attending Bengali school: '[O]bviously my family speak Bangla and I spoke Bangla there and you know English at school but it was never separated so we spoke a bit of both ... it's all mixed up, I mean I don't think I can speak a Bangla sentence without adding English in it.' Hasna used these skills for displays where she had written words in Bangla, 'but not often and maybe I should do it more. I don't think I do it often enough.' She also used a lot of Bangla in the classroom, especially in the early years when settling new children who had no command of English into school: '[I]t's a way of making them feel secure, comfortable you know ... it's a really good thing that they come in and see home link already ... with teachers that are not bilingual they find it difficult and the children find it frustrating.' In her view, some of the non-Bangladeshi teachers found it quite frustrating that the child didn't always understand them. Usually, she found this was easily resolved as teachers developed an understanding of body language. They also resorted to using visual resources, which usually worked. The children tended to be more relaxed: '[T]hey learn from each other really, they end up playing coz I think for them that's not a big issue.'

Hasna describes the current school she was working at as having just over 50 per cent Bangladeshi children and the rest from various backgrounds. She was pleased as most other schools in Tower Hamlets were 99 per cent Bangladeshi. She appreciated the cultural mix compared to other schools and it was good for the children, as it enabled more integration. The school also had the only Bangladeshi head teacher in the borough. Hasna thought that made a difference for the parents, as they were able to look up to a person who was from the community and was well respected, but that it made little difference as far as the children were concerned. The children saw him as they saw the other teachers but, at the same time, they were able to relate to him a little more, and she identified with this herself, saying:

> Even me as a class teacher they kind of just accept it but what's nice as a class teacher being bilingual myself is that they can relate, you can kind of end up bringing a lot of home into the classroom and talk a lot about the classroom and then I can share my experiences and then they kind of get excited.
>
> Hasna, Aminah and Samiha's teacher

Her own schooling experience was very different:

> We had a few more English speaking children there ... but the system was different, the system was like free flow a lot of topic work, a lot of topic-based work, lots of creative work and ehm now I feel the system has changed and it is very structured, teachers teach and children learning although it is supposed to be like a bit of both I think in practice in terms of what's required of us as teachers we end up having to make it sort of really structured.
>
> Hasna

Hasna engaged with parents by initiating regular contact outside the timetabled parent–child meetings to discuss the progress of their children and to see where and how the parents could support their learning:

> Bengali parents definitely aren't that confident to come to the teacher so I would go up to them coz I know they're not very

confident with the language and I'll speak in Bangla … the parents that are interested you can tell coz you know parents that sort of like encourage children to take books … even though I know there are parents that aren't interested I will still go to those parents and just push, push, push, just because I know that they're not interested and I will make myself known to them and say, look you know as a teacher you kind of end up doing that anyway and its not that it's like I guess because I dunno maybe somehow because I'm Bengali I probably kind of like push them a bit more.

Hasna

Hasna was aware that many of the parents at the school were not literate in English, and her fellow teachers often commented that these were the parents who were not interested in their children's education. However, she made an effort to engage and speak to these parents by encouraging them:

I usually say to the parents, 'I know you can't read but the simple thing of just sitting with your child with the book and letting them do the reading and they'll do the talking is really actually good as long as you're actually sitting there with them and they get the physical contact and they are talking, even in Bangla.'

Hasna

In order to promote children's learning in school, Hasna felt teachers should really get to know them, to know where they come from and what they were like at home:

Once they can identify themselves as a person then they can start relating to things ehm … then they just make it a bigger picture like whenever I do a village life in India it's basically India, but then I would change it to Bangladesh coz it is a contrasting locality, I would just change it to Bangladesh coz the children can relate to it and they also at the same time talk about India because it is very close to Bangladesh, and do it like that and so I would refer to the children and even when there's like an English child from a different background, and again when teaching RE I can do that quite easily 'what do you do at home and do you go to church' that kind of thing.

Hasna

However, in her view, the curriculum did not allow teachers to incorporate this easily as it 'doesn't really give an opportunity for the children to identify themselves', unless teachers were creative and used the circle times to allow children to explore ideas and share information about themselves:

> I can't remember the last lesson where we actually did work on ourselves, I mean we do have topics on ourselves and then that's where we look at the environment, we look at our family but then its more topic related and its not everything else.
>
> Hasna

When asked whether she had the opportunity to consult research and its value in supporting professional development, Hasna replied:

> Research? – no ehm I think yeah it would (help) I think it would also help other teachers like us being bilingual, it would help other teachers think and talk about some of the cultures I think, ehm at the moment most of the teachers have adopted a kind of very negative sort of ok yeah parents aren't very interested and speak Bangla, is all quite negative.
>
> Hasna

And finally, describing Aminah:

> … ehm I would say with Aminah I know that her parents are kind of like they speak Bangla and they're bilingual and what you call like today's kind of couple, where they speak English, they both got jobs … so they're kind of very established here really, so Aminah herself she's very kind of confident because of all that. Also she does a lot of extracurricular activities and things so I think because of that that's really helped and she's also quite an able child, she kind of picks up on things quite quick … quite good at everything … quite sporty, she's an all-rounder.
>
> Hasna

Hasna's description of Samiha was rather different:

> … ehm Samiha is very bubbly very chatty ehm she's got a really good sense of humour, and ehm academically she's not that able … she is also very sporty so there's that … but I think she lacks in confidence and she isn't very able, she quite like finds it hard to read and has difficulty writing as well, although you know for her she's done very well she has kind of picked up the confidence and ehm, I think more a SEN case so she does have some difficulty. I don't know if it's family related or just learning or an emotional

thing I don't know. Samiha I think it's slightly different because her mum, I don't think is very academic coz she got married quite young as well ehm and as a result her mum doesn't speak really good English. Samiha's English isn't that great but that's not always the case – my mum didn't speak English and you know I speak English, but I was encouraged, my dad used to encourage and I have siblings that would encourage so I think with Samiha ... do you know I can't remember, she's got her uncles I think. Yeah and ehm can't remember if she's got any brothers and sisters she's got a little sister ... she lives with the extended family with her grandparents.

Hasna

Jade, Habib's teacher

Jade was Habib's class teacher, white British, in her early thirties and had been teaching for the last ten years. She had graduated with a B.A. in Education in primary years and had worked in schools in Devon, Birmingham, and London. Being born and raised in Devon, her experience of schooling was hardly multicultural, though 'we did have people from other cultures but they were literally single people from one single cultural background'. When working in Birmingham and London, one of her biggest worries was communicating with parents and she was very aware then that her language skills were inadequate. So, Jade believed that teaching definitely required cultural knowledge and she had since been able to acquire that knowledge through building relationships with parents and other members of staff who were from different cultural backgrounds, 'who have been brilliant coz I can come and ask them questions without feeling too silly and likewise they can ask me things'.

Although Jade said that the PGCE training could never fully prepare a teacher trainee to becoming culturally aware, she did appreciate the opportunity to have inner-city placements in Birmingham and London, where, she said,

I was able to address that early on and then I knew that when lectures came up about bilingual learning I was also able to say ... some of my children speak different languages and actually the lecturers would then adapt sort of personalized sessions more. And again in London they gave us quite a lot before if they knew we were coming to do a London placement. We did have an optional series of lectures to attend ... we had one lecturer who was like you will learn more being in the area, living in the area working and talking with the people of that area than you will learn from me in this room in Devon and I liked that.

Jade, Habib's teacher

This insight helped Jade to think more carefully about the context of the children's lives compared to her own, as she believed there were differences in her experience of childhood and the experiences the children had. One of the experiences was being able to speak other languages:

They have two languages going on, they have a school language and a home language and they are able to interchange and you know that is helpful having other people to support me in sharing what that feels like and making sure that I am aware.

Jade

However, she has noticed that in her previous class not many children used their home language in the classroom:

I also have a Japanese speaking child and he is the one that switched most frequently from Japanese to English than my Bangla speakers, they like to speak English, well they give me that impression that they like to speak English at school but they are happy to speak their other language at home.

Jade

Jade observed that when the children were younger they were comfortable and happy to share their cultural and religious experiences with her. She tried to give them lots of opportunities to talk about what was happening in their homes, their celebrations and festivals. The Muslim children liked to share stories of Eid celebrations, and a Russian girl talked about what they did for St Nicholas celebrations. The school had become more diverse in the previous three to four years:

It's been absolutely super seeing children integrating far more naturally and ehm with that actually, children who may have difficulties with the language and who may be seen as quieter and shyer are starting to bring in a little photograph or saying 'I've celebrated this as well' especially with Eid or Ramadhan 'my mum is fasting, my big brothers are waking up in the night to pray' and we have lots of books to support that ehm try to have stories both fiction and information to support.

Jade

However, she noticed that older children became more self-conscious and they worried more about the importance of their heritage and questioned its position in their lives:

> I don't know why but I do think there might be some developmental side to it, it's to do with body awareness you know, they all have that big hormone surge between year 6 to 7 and as they move on into juniors there is a sudden awareness about their body, about the space they take up about the fact that who's grown who's not, whose teeth are falling out, whose teeth are not falling out, and I think possibly that physical change possibly impacts at some level on their cultural identity as well and they may associate some things to their culture they may not, for me I can say for my cultural background what I have brought with me, my insecurities … but I do think that with all of that development thing that possibly this is the age where we begin to see that they are slightly nervous, they start to work out a hierarchy … they sort of work it out and you know they find their place.
>
> Jade

Jade stressed the importance of her role within her diverse class, to celebrate and promote everyone's cultural heritage and diversity, 'we're the same and we're different', and celebrating the differences. She and her colleagues shared a lot of resources to deliver knowledge in a wider context so that everyone's history and cultural diversity was recognized. They tried consciously, even when they put on shows and concerts at the end of term:

> … like we've got this celebration concert called a 'Christmassy concert' and I know some teachers are singing in different languages, we've got Y6 doing ehm Alexandra books halleluiah but in Arabic … a mambo from Mexico just a chance to bring different cultures to show the children that actually we're all same but different and we celebrate that.
>
> Jade

When Jade planned work for the children in her class one of her key strategies was to look for something that they were interested in, particularly when there was a broader topic during a term. One such example was when they were covering the topic of forces. She encouraged the children to bring in vehicles and even within that there were a group of boys who wanted to look at helicopters. Because she invested her time at the beginning of the term to find out what they were interested in, she was, she said,

... able to adapt sort of the skills and the knowledge that are required to teach them and gear in things that I know they'll be interested in as well to keep them motivated and engaged ... so that children are more accountable for their personal learning so it's not about the able ones that will always answer the questions ... actually everyone is expected to make a contribution and that's been very positive.

Jade

Also, small individual whiteboards were used, which Jade felt encouraged personal learning, 'so people don't feel like everyone's looking, they can just write down the answer and they can show it to me and my eyes and their eyes and they don't have to share it'.

Jade believed the key aspects to building the children's academic identity was for them to experience success, which would enable them to build their own self-esteem. This success was an accumulation of smaller successful steps and, in celebrating that success with them, she felt their academic level moved up with parental support, which should include an honest appraisal and approach, 'and if it is home and school then that child really flies ehm they need to feel safe, confident as learners and as people and if you get that, it's those children who are usually successful'. Jade tended to use the parent and child conference to gauge the adults that supported the children with their learning at home: '[I]t doesn't matter who they do it with [laughs] someone anyone as long as it's done!' However, she did stress that she couldn't confidently say for every child specifically who it was that supported them at home as she felt there were certain constraints on teachers, preventing them from finding out more about the home. One such constraint was the curriculum, which she described as quite prescriptive:

You have to be creative, I certainly will eh uhm [struggles a little] I bend rules ... break rules to fit my class, that's quite a core belief of mine ... this belief has grown as I've grown as a teacher ... possibly for the last two years I'm at my strongest on its right for my children and they're learning. Then we do it and if it's not right then I'll pay lip service to it and tick the box and we'll move on quickly, but I do think that especially with certain topics that we are obliged to teach it ... it's more usually with the skill-based [learning] then I'm not and I don't feel I'm in a box having to teach something and I feel like we can apply the skills more widely.

Jade

When asked to reflect on whether she had the opportunity to read and consult research in order to aid professional development, Jade responded: 'not as many as we would like'. She was part of the Association of Science Educators and subscribed to a scientific journal:

> ... and during the holidays I tend to catch up [laughs], I am science and technology lead, so I feel like that as the senior leader for that I should have a deeper understanding of what I'm asking people to do ehm we often share articles on INSET days so ehm and I know TES, that's what a lot of teachers buy that are into primary education and they get a lot of their information ... but probably compared to what we do at university and the level it isn't the same and you don't have the time to digest ... when I get the chance it does help and I'm always interested in thinking about what people are still finding out about.
>
> Jade

Jade's reflection on Habib:

> Well ... Habib is a quiet but confident child ehm he likes to learn but needs to be set little targets where he can feel he is succeeding ... he's a clever boy ehm haven't really heard him speak any other language but I know mum's a teacher and she speaks English ... the grandmother? [laughs] she came on our trip last year [saying with pride] it was brilliant ehm when she talks she's very smiley and she has been on our trips and I know she helps mum with her childcare and I know she's quite supportive in the home especially with the new baby, so I was sort of aware on that level and I think mum and dad do a lot more of the home work and the learning that's my sort of understanding of it.
>
> Jade

Both teachers stated the importance of understanding children's backgrounds. However, they observed that this often was not possible due to constraints of time and curriculum targets. Hasna used her knowledge of her own community to reach out to parents and Jade relied on teachers like Hasna to understand some of the cultural aspects of the children in her class. Although Hasna shared a similar upbringing to Samiha, as her own parents didn't speak much English, I expected her to understand Samiha's learning environment but, surprisingly, she suggested that Samiha's learning and social development was affected negatively by her family dynamics.

Her perceptions of both Samiha and Aminah were based on the lifestyle maintained by the parents and the extended family of the two girls. Hasna saw Aminah as more academic and a high achiever, as her parents facilitated more extracurricular activities for her and were 'today's' image of hard-working parents. This is similar to the impression held by the teacher mentioned in Kenner *et al.*'s (2007) study of the children in his class. Hasna, on the other hand, based her assessment of Samiha on her limited knowledge of the interactions taking place between Samiha and the members of her extended family at home. Hasna's assumptions were unexpected as she shared the same cultural and faith background as the two girls; parents would normally expect her to have a more open view of Samiha's context. Turn-taking and question-and-answer patterns revealed more about the nature of the interactions between the children and their teachers.

Turn-taking and question-and-answer patterns

Hasna sat with Aminah and Samiha in her classroom to put the puzzles together. On each occasion, the activity took place during break, while the other children played outside. On a separate visit to the school, Jade and Habib's mother agreed to him doing the puzzle one evening after school. Habib and Jade sat next to each other at a table in their classroom. Table 4.1 below shows the details of the puzzle each pair engaged in, the time taken and the total number of turns taken to complete them:

Table 4.1: Record of puzzles and time taken to complete them by each child–teacher pair

	Aminah & Teacher (Hasna)	Samiha & Teacher (Hasna)	Habib & Teacher (Jade)
Name of Puzzle	UK and the Republic of Ireland Map	Solar System	UK and the Republic of Ireland Map
No. of Pieces	100-piece puzzle featuring places of interest from around the United Kingdom and Republic of Ireland	60-piece puzzle featuring the names of all the planets in the solar system	100-piece puzzle featuring places of interest from around the United Kingdom and Republic of Ireland
Time Taken	29:13 mins	32:52 mins	40:56 mins
Total No. of Turns (Verbal & Non-Verbal)	366	693	869

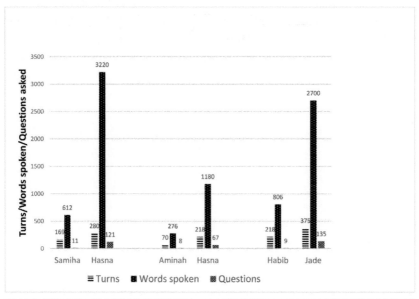

Participant	Number of Verbal Turns	Number of Words Spoken	Questions Asked by Each Participant
Samiha	169	612	11
Hasna	280	3220	121
Aminah	70	276	8
Hasna	218	1180	67
Habib	218	806	9
Jade	375	2700	135

Figure 4.1: Breakdown of the number of verbal turns, the number of words spoken, and the number of questions asked by each participant in the child–teacher pairs

The data is used to compare the child-to-teacher ratio with the child-to-mother and child-to-grandmother ratios (see table 4.2) to investigate the similarities, differences, and patterns of interaction during the shared activity.

Figure 4.1 shows (both as a graph and in numbers) that the number of turns taken by the teachers was approximately twice that of the children. Also, Hasna spoke four times as many words as Aminah, and five times more than Samiha. Jade spoke three times more words than Habib did throughout the activity. The striking evidence for the authority the teachers had during the activities was demonstrated by the sheer number of questions they asked, compared to those asked by the children. During their activity,

Hasna managed to ask 67 questions and Aminah only 8. The ratio of words per turn spoken by the teachers was twice as many as that of the children, with Hasna speaking approximately three times more than Samiha during their shared activity. The children's ratio of words spoken per turn revealed that each child spoke approximately four words per turn, thus their turns were very short.

Table 4.2: Ratios of verbal turns, words per turn, words and questions asked in each child–teacher pair

	Teacher (Hasna) & Samiha	Teacher (Hasna) & Aminah	Teacher (Jade) & Habib
Ratio of Turns Teacher/Child	280/169 = 1.7	141/70 = 2.0	375/218 = 1.7
Ratio of Words Per Turn	Samiha: 612/169=3.6 Hasna: 3220/280=11.5	Aminah: 276/70=3.9 Hasna: 1180/141=7.8	Habib: 806/218=3.5 Jade: 2700/375=6.5
Ratio of Words Teacher/Child	3220/612 = 5.3	1180/276 = 4.3	2700/806 = 3.3
Ratio of Questions Teacher/Child	121/11 = 11	67/8 = 8.4	135/9 = 15

It became obvious when looking at the transcripts across all the pairs that turn-taking did not always take place as expected, with one speaker talking at a time and turns being taken with as little gap or overlap as possible between them. In the child–teacher pairs (Table 4.3), the teachers tended to dominate the turns, sometimes taking several turns consecutively.

Table 4.3: Number of consecutive turns taken by each child and their teacher

Number of consecutive turns	2	3	4	5	6	7	8	9
Teacher (Hasna)	43	16	9	3	1	1		
Samiha	8	1						
Teacher (Jade)	32	21	10	3	5	1	2	
Habib	5							
Teacher (Hasna)	21	15	4	1		1		
Aminah	2							

Table 4.4 presents a breakdown of the types of questions asked by the children and their teachers during the activity.

Table 4.4: Child–teacher pair: non-redundant, redundant, and self-responses

	Samiha	Teacher (Hasna)	Aminah	Teacher (Hasna)	Habib	Teacher (Jade)
No. of Non-Redundant Questions	10	55	20	27	17	70
No. of Redundant Questions	3	28	2	27	4	26
No. of Self-Response Questions	5	30	3	12	3	30
% of Redundant and Self-Response Questions	44%	51%	20%	59%	29%	44%

Table 4.4 reflects the fact that the teachers talked more and they held the floor more consistently. Many of the consecutive turns taken were in the form of questions directed at the children (Transcript, Examples 1, 2, and 3 below). These were frequent and the teachers expected the children to respond with brief answers. This was demanding at times and often created confusion as the children tried to work out which question to respond to, alongside trying to put the puzzle together. This produced a high percentage of redundant questions and the teachers responding to their own questions. However, when the children asked questions, the teachers did respond to them.

The first example below (Example 1) is a portion of the transcript of the interaction between Jade and Habib during the activity. Jade had a deeper understanding of what she could expect from her pupils, as she had gained valuable training and experience from her participation in a research programme exploring ways to assist and develop children's learning. During this training, there were opportunities for her to find out about other research studies as well as consult journals and other publications. Jade also followed the research study by Kenner *et al.* (2004b) held at the school by reading some of the published articles and speaking to colleagues who were involved. Jade and Habib take 869 moves in total to complete their puzzle.

Although Jade makes attempts to allow Habib to take the lead throughout the activity, her role as the knowledgeable teacher was very visible.

EXAMPLE 1 (child–teacher pair: H: Habib and J: Jade)

1. ((H has the box and contemplates what to do))
2. J: what you going to do?
3. J: what is the puzzle of?
4. H: the the <u>WORLD</u>?
5. ((H looks up at J))
6. ((J looks at the puzzle))
7. J: the <u>world</u>?

In this interaction, Jade initiated the activity, defining who was in charge by asking Habib two consecutive questions (turns 2 and 3) that required different responses. She was expecting him to read the title of the puzzle from the box but he responded by saying what he thought it was after looking at the picture of the map on the box (turn 4). She pursued this and unpicked it with Habib, taking a further 19 turns until he was able to read the whole title of the puzzle from the box.

26. H: Republic of Ireland
27. J: super! and that's the island
28. (..)
29. ((J points to the box and circles the part of Ireland with her finger))
30. J: there so we gonna be looking at that <u>RIGHT</u>! Where shall we <u>start</u>?

Jade closes the sequence by praising Habib (turn 27) and in turn 30 she suggests indirectly using the box as a reference, which she establishes in turn 45 (below). When Habib turns down Jade's offer to help him (turns 47–52), she still takes on the role of the guide by asking him what their plan was for starting the activity. This discussion around which pieces to select and how to move forward continues between turns 57–70.

45. J: so you're using the box to help us <u>aren't you</u>?
46. ((H nods yes))
47. J: can I is there anything I can do to help <u>you with it</u>?
48. H: °uhm°
49. (0.5)
50. H: °no°
51. ((H nods his head))

52. J: <u>no</u>?
53. ((J nods her head, too))
54. J: ok what's our plan to go first?
55. J: to do what are we looking for first?
56. ((They both look at the box))

Throughout the activity, Jade coaxed Habib into interacting verbally and non-verbally, but she remained in control of the topics and decided on the shifts and changes, as can be seen between turns 71–77 below. Jade introduced a topic that could potentially have opened up a conversation that allowed her to share a bit more about her life and Habib to share more about his, but the conversation ended and Jade shifted it back to the task at hand.

71. J: see that one that's where I was <u>born</u>
72. ((J points to a piece, smiles and looks at H))
73. (0.4)
74. J: in that town
75. (..)
76. J: Ipswich that's funny I didn't know that would be on there
77. ((J folds back her arms))

We see how the turns were initiated by Jade, at times with closed questions. The responses were often short and, when Habib's responses matched what Jade wanted to hear, she almost always followed them up with positive celebratory feedback such as 'super' and 'brilliant', and sometimes added explanations as in turn 88:

88. J: I like your plan for starting with sides

Below is the transcript of Hasna and Aminah completing the puzzle. It took 56 out of the 366 verbal and non-verbal moves before Aminah and Hasna actually started their activity. Although Aminah made an initiating statement (turn 2), she did not speak again until she replied to Hasna's question (turn 8).

EXAMPLE 2 (child–teacher pair: A: Aminah and H: Hasna)

1. ((A and H look at the picture of the map on the box))
2. A: °there's a map°
3. ((H is holding up the box))
4. ((A looks at the picture on the box of the map))
5. H: so it's the <u>British</u>?

6.   (.)
7.   H: <u>Isles</u>
8.   H: did you do that in <u>year 2</u>?

Turns 9–47 were dominated by Hasna, and Aminah responded very briefly. Hasna, like Jade, also suggested using the box as a guide (turn 15). The verbal moves tended to be test questions or statements directed at Aminah asking her how best to approach the activity (turn 17 below). Although Aminah answered (turn 20), Hasna seemed to go off on a tangent again by repeating the same question in different ways (turns 23–24). And Hasna did not respond to Aminah when she made a concrete suggestion on how to start the activity (turn 20).

15.   H: alright so we gonna <u>try</u> and <u>use</u> the box as our picture.
16.   (..)
17.   H: do you want to tell me what to do first?
18.   ((H closes up the box and places it at arm's length away from them))
19.   ((They both look at the box))
20.   A: you have to find the °name and we need to find the edges°
21.   ((A points at the map on the box))
22.   ((A and H both still look at the box))
23.   H: do you know how best to do a <u>jigsaw</u>?
24.   H: have you done a jigsaw <u>before</u>?

Hasna also tended to ask questions, taking consecutive turns that Aminah sometimes found difficult to respond to (turns 23, 24). Between turns 25–44 Hasna asked whether Aminah was good at doing puzzles and how difficult she found them. This involved Hasna asking Aminah questions, and only twice did Aminah have the opportunity to answer. This was reflected in the 59 per cent redundant and self-response questions on Hasna's part and demonstrated when Hasna asked the two questions (turns 48 and 49) and Aminah was left confused (turns 50 and 51). Rather than allowing Aminah a bit more time, Hasna went on to answer her own questions (turn 52), and Aminah listened attentively.

45.   H: >how shall we do this?<
46.   H: >are you going to do a part or are we going to do it together?<
47.   A: together
48.   H: right have you got any ideas of how quickly we can do this?

49. H: r shall we just take our time?
50. A: eh eh eh
51. ((A looks lost for words laughs and nods her head, slightly confused))
52. H: I've got an idea what we can do is we can group it so we can look at the colours so look this is quite good so look we've got all the pinks, all the yellows, then we got all the blues and here are all the greens then we'll know what colours to do what you can do is first group all the colours before we start to stick bits together and if you <u>do</u> see something you <u>can</u> fit it together let's group all the colours first

Hasna, like Jade, praised Aminah when she managed to follow her lead:

140. H: oh good girl so this bit goes here and that bit there and how about this?

Hasna's way to guide Aminah through the activity was to ask questions. However, Aminah did not reply to many of them and, when she did, Hasna failed to follow through on her responses as can be seen in the following section of the transcript. Aminah did not challenge this but moved along with Hasna and complied with her teacher's suggestions. She did the same when Hasna used the opportunity to link the activity to the geography curriculum topic they covered (turns 162–164).

150. H: how <u>do you</u> do your jigsaws at home?
151. A: I dunno I just find the main bits and put them in the middle
152. H: ahh so you find the main bits so what would be the main bits?
153. H: here?
154. ((H points to the picture on the box and circles it with her finger))
155. A: hmm the flag bits
156. ((A points to the picture, too))
157. H: would that <u>be the main bits</u>?
158. H: it would be that wouldn't it?
159. H: so shall we start to put the pinks together?
160. A: here's a pink
161. (...)

162. H: and we can use a bit of geography here as well couldn't
     <u>you</u> coz look here's all the names of the places so <u>you</u> can
     guess <u>where</u> places are so we can find
163. A: that's London
164. H: so let's find London

It took Hasna and Samiha (Example 3) 69 moves out of a total of 693 verbal and non-verbal moves before they started to put pieces together. The nature of conversation was very similar to the previous two examples. It was very much based around the technicalities of finding the right pieces and putting them together. Here, too, Hasna asked numerous questions, of which 51 per cent were self-responses and questions that were redundant.

EXAMPLE 3 (child–teacher pair: H: Hasna and S: Samiha)

1. H: () puzzle <u>look</u> can you <u>read it</u>?
2. ((H shows the picture on the box to S))
3. S: the
4. (..)
5. S: solar system
6. H: >the solar system so what do you think this puzzle's
    going to be about?<
7. S: about the solar [system]
8. H: [how] [oh] ( ) I'm just opening the box do you want
    to open it?

Although Hasna remained in control of both conversations, the turns developed such that conversational equality was greater in the interchange between Hasna and Aminah than in the one between Hasna and Samiha. Although Aminah and Hasna did not get to complete the activity, in a similar amount of time Hasna asked Samiha approximately twice as many questions (Figure 4.1), and these were more direct and testing (e.g. turns 1 and 6), as Hasna was assessing whether Samiha could read by herself and gauging her knowledge of what the puzzle was about (turns 1–8). This could have been because Hasna thought Samiha needed more assistance and prompting, believing that Samiha lacked academic support at home. With Aminah, on the other hand, Hasna read out the title of the puzzle herself, which again reinforces her view of Aminah being more academically capable. Hasna also had twice as many turns in this conversation than in the conversation between her and Aminah (Table 4.4).

Turns 9–26 continued in a similar manner, Hasna asking many questions and giving directions. The following portion of the transcript shows the style of questioning to be directive and imperative (turns 27, 29–30, 32).

21. H: so what do you think is the best way to sort a puzzle out?
22. S: °( )°
23. H: what a good <u>idea</u> so let's get all the right colours together so you choose all the white bits and then I'll choose <u>the so what colours</u>?
24. H: help me choose what [colours?]
25. S: °[hmm]°
26. H: what <u>colour</u> shall I choose?
27. S: you can choose all the green bits
28. H: I'll take all the green bits
29. S: aliens

Below, Hasna starts off by taking on Samiha's suggestion (turn 48) and discusses solutions, with Samiha complying diligently. However, by turn 59 Hasna changed her mind.

48. H: [so we] shall we get <u>the alien first</u>?
49. H: ok you get the alien °and I'll get the astronaut° that's and I'll you pass me <u>my alien</u> bits if you see any alien bits you pass to me
50. S: °yeah°
51. H: >and then if I see any astronaut bits I'll pass to you<
52. S: °[ok]°
53. H: [that looks] like a something what do you think that is?
54. S: °I think that's an alien°
55. H: °ok°
56. ((S tries to put pieces together herself))
57. ((H gets on with her pieces))
58. (0.4)
59. H: I changed my mind I'm going to go for <u>the rocket</u> coz it's <u>easier</u>

Samiha was more talkative by nature than Aminah but said very little and there were hardly any instances where she carried the discussion further, introduced a topic, asked any questions that interested her or generally talked about her own interests. I believe one of the reasons for this difference in interaction was the differing perceptions the teacher held of the children. Hasna had told me during her interview that Samiha did not have a family environment that contained many learning opportunities, so felt she was struggling academically, whereas she felt that Aminah had all the support from home she required to achieve her full academic potential. This shaped the way Hasna interacted with Samiha and Aminah during the activities.

It is evident from the three transcripts and Tables 4.3 and 4.4 that in all three situations communication was firmly centred on the teachers. It was they who talked and decided when the children could talk; it was the teachers who asked the questions, evaluated the answers, and managed the sequences as a whole. There was also a pattern of teachers asking a number of questions in one go and not providing an opportunity for the children to respond. The children rarely asked questions about what the teacher meant or requested them to elaborate on their meanings. The children tended to accept that what they did manage to say in answer to the teacher's questions would almost certainly be evaluated (by repetition, the teacher's own suggestions or questions), might well be interrupted if the teacher judged it irrelevant to her purposes, and might be modified and translated to fit the teacher's frame of reference. In the above transcript, Hasna and Samiha went through a discussion about where to start the activity, the possibilities ranging from colours to characters. Just as they got to a point of agreement in turn 59, Hasna decided to change her mind. Since the teachers usually know the right answers or give the impression that they do, the children learn to focus on the many clues and cues the teacher provides to narrow the search area for the pieces and the number of possible ways forward. Their task was to respond, rarely to initiate, and, although at times the teachers did take on ideas from the children, they did generally decide on the best way to deal with the shared endeavour and what the children should achieve from the activity.

That said, the child–teacher pairs did manage to complete the shared endeavours, except for Aminah and Hasna, for whom time ran out. The children participated, the teachers were scaffolding the children's learning through their ZPD to reach their Zone of Actual Development (ZAD), which was to put the pieces of puzzles together. But they restricted the children's participation. An important aspect of scaffolding during these activities was that the children felt successful in their endeavour. The greatest probability of student success is achieved when challenging tasks are matched with a high level of support. For all the children, this was their first or second attempt at putting a puzzle together, and they were able to complete the challenging task with assistance from their teachers, with the children playing the novices.

The next chapter explores intergenerational learning between children and their mothers and compares this with the learning between children and their teachers.

Chapter 5

Exploring intergenerational learning between children and their mothers

The interviews with the mothers revealed the way Layla, Shamima, and Thamima approach learning and their part in their children's learning, juggling the roles of being a mother and educator and facilitating the role the grandmothers play in the lives of their children. This chapter presents data that demonstrates the mothers' views and practices, against the backdrop of previous studies investigating children's learning at home.

The transcripts and the patterns of interaction between the mothers and the children highlight that mostly guided participation was used by the mothers during the jigsaw puzzle endeavours. We can see the often demanding position of the mothers who are juggling the expectations from the school and the home. However, it is the ways in which children engage with their mothers that are most interesting, and these become clearer when turn-taking and question-and-answer patterns are explored.

Children's learning at home

> They love going to her house they drive me crazy sometimes!
> She's got so ... this much to give ... she's she's free well makes
> herself free for them, coz I work I find I'm tired and stressed,
> always other things on my mind, course I try but you know how
> it is [sighs].
>
> > Rashida, mother: Pilot study

The next part of the interview transcript demonstrates how the mother aspired to take on the role of a teacher:

> Well I did childcare and work with children so I can learn better
> ways of teaching my children. I see the way children learn and
> I want to give the same to my own ehm my mum didn't have
> the same opportunities she just left us to it [laughs], he takes it
> seriously with me [smiling], but with her he learns all the cultural
> stuff you know ehm, so she can relax, actually I probably stress

him out sometimes and he likes it with *nani* no demands, no pressure just love love [laughs].

Rashida

There has been increasing recognition within developmental, educational, and sociological theories that school and home are both important institutions in socializing and educating children. As Gregory suggests, '[i]f we take seriously the evidence that a child interprets the world in a way consistent with the home culture, we must look to find ways by which we both acknowledge that culture and introduce children explicitly to the new world they are entering in school' (Gregory, 1994: 121). This issue has risen to the top of the political agenda in the last three decades (Cremin and Drury, 2015).

Schools frequently specify what parents can do to support their children's learning at home based on school instructions, rather than seeing the home as a source of complementary literacy and learning experiences (Crozier and Davies, 2007). To clarify the role of the learner in their cognitive development within the framework of sociocultural theory, Rogoff (1990), a neo-Vygotskian, introduced the term 'guided participation' within a community context. Note that scaffolding and guided participation, sometimes used interchangeably, contrast with traditional views of learning, where it is assumed that the learner is separated from the environmental context in which the learning is taking place. Although the terms are often used interchangeably, guided participation leans more towards active involvement from the novice than scaffolding the activity within the social context of the home in which learning is occurring (Rogoff, 1990; Stone, 1998). Guided participation occurs throughout the life course of a child as they progress from a peripheral and dependent role to greater independence and responsibility through working to master the challenges posed by their social and cultural surroundings (Rogoff, 1990; Gauvain, 2001).

Children are seen to participate actively with others as 'more skilled partners and their challenging and exploring peers' (Rogoff, 1990: 8), who serve as both guides and collaborators. Together they draw upon cultural resources and build on what children know and can do to co-construct learning. The practices, routines, and talk that occur within these settings are important because they reveal the interactions and understandings of the participants (Heath, 1991; Wertsch, 1985).

We know that parents in different parts of the world have different expectations about learning and social practices for themselves and their children, according to the cultural norms within which they are functioning.

Harkness and Super (1992) compared the words contained in parental talk about children in two cultural settings: metropolitan America and rural Kenya. They observed that the American children were far more verbally precocious and adept at imaginative play than the Kenyan children. On the other hand, the Kenyan children were able to shoulder huge familial responsibilities such as taking care of younger siblings and cooking for the whole family at the age of 8.

These issues have been substantiated by findings from cross-cultural research by Rogoff *et al.* (1993), comparing parent–toddler pairs from four cultural settings: Mayans in Mexico, Salt Lake City in the USA, Turkey, and India. The main focus of the findings was a comparison of just two early childhood contexts, parents and children in Mayan communities and in Salt Lake City. During the ethnographic analysis, the authors became aware of similarities and differences in the two communities in efforts to bridge the toddlers' and mothers' understandings of the situation and to structure the toddlers' involvement. The findings showed that guided participation includes similarities in two important processes: 'creating bridges' to make connections to new ideas and skills and 'structuring children's participation' in activities where opportunities are created for them to be involved, during which social support is provided. The activities were challenging and the roles given to the children were in line with those valued in their community (Rogoff *et al.*, 1998).

The differences Rogoff and her team observed between the US mother–child pairs and the Mexican Mayan mother–child pairs in their homes were in the way they interacted with selected materials, such as a baby doll, nesting dolls (a set of wooden dolls that fit one inside the other), and play dough. They found that the middle-class North American parents and others with similar schooling experiences appeared to place more emphasis on verbal interaction and statements. When they did speak, they gave indirect instructions. The most significant difference between the pairs was in the emphasis each placed on the status of the child, with the American child 'being treated as the object of teaching and the Mayan child being responsible for learning' (Rogoff *et al.*, 1998: 246). They highlighted the ways in which the mothers interacted with and assisted their children. The American caregivers tended to act as teachers and playmates whereas the Mayan mothers expressed readiness to aid their children's efforts to learn (246–7).

Patterns of interaction

> Children learn by apprenticing: by watching, learning, practicing, mimicking, transforming and absorbing the ways with words used in the social sites by those around them. Everyday life is thus a complex fabric of speech events, where that apprenticeship takes place ... To make meaning we adhere to (and regularly stretch and break) social conventions, which dictate who can speak when, how, about what – when to be silent, what is an appropriate comment, how to take turns in conversations, who has more power in talk, gesture and other aspects of communication.
>
> Luke and Kale, 1997: 13

Conversations are usually governed by rules and they often seek certain goals, depending on the cultural context and the nature of the sociocultural activities the participants are involved in. One reason why talk-in-interaction is such a good place for observing methods of sense-making is because it systematically requires the listeners to attend to what speakers are saying and to come to and display some understanding of it.

Aminah, Samiha, and Habib act similarly to those referred to by Luke and Kale (1997: 9): 'Different cultures make meaning in different ways, with different patterns of exchange and interaction. The children learn to live in different worlds/multiple worlds to switch from one language/ literacy practice to another, each with its corresponding set of rules.' They live in multiple worlds or 'simultaneous worlds' (Kenner, 2004), where patterns of exchanges and interactions are different. They are the agents that often transmit the knowledge and experiences between these worlds. The difference, however, with these third-generation British Bangladeshi children, is that they entered school already familiar with the language and behaviour rituals, or 'recipes' (Hymes, 1974) of the classroom, unlike the children referred to by Luke and Kale. This familiarity was passed on from the parents' experiences of going to school in Britain and sharing this with their children. Also, in all three cases, the families shared the practice of reading stories at home and were using appropriate, socially accepted linguistic recipes, e.g., 'please' and 'thank you', etc. and are speakers of the language and members of the culture represented and validated in their schools. My study supports and expands on the studies by Kenner *et al.* (2004b, 2007) in highlighting that these children entered classrooms possessing additional knowledge and etiquettes that can be seen as additional 'recipes' that are not expected in school alongside the accepted 'recipes' recognized by teachers.

Turn-taking and question-and-answer patterns

Samiha and her mother both sat on the living room floor with Surayah, Samiha's younger sister, and Akhter, their paternal first cousin. He was present at the beginning and joined the activity again later at Samiha's request. Aminah and her mother sat side by side on the small floor space in a bedroom at Aminah's grandmother's house. Habib and his mother sat opposite one another on the floor of Habib's aunt's room, along with Habib's younger sister and his grandmother. The details of the puzzles and the length of time taken to complete them are shown in the Table 5.1 below:

Table 5.1: Record of puzzles and times taken to complete them by each child–mother pair

	Aminah & Mother (Layla)	Samiha & Mother (Shamima)	Habib & Mother (Thaminah)
Name of Puzzle	Solar System	Jungle Floor Puzzle	Solar System
No. of Pieces	60-piece puzzle featuring the names of all the planets in the solar system	24-piece puzzle featuring a cartoon jungle scene with lots of creatures	60-piece puzzle featuring the names of all the planets in the solar system
Time Taken	15:48 mins	11:36 mins	15:29 mins
Total No. of Turns (Verbal & Non-Verbal)	373	494	488

The numerical values in Figure 5.1 indicate an approximately equal number of turns taken by child and mother. Habib and Samiha also utter a similar number of words to their mothers. However, Aminah's mother spoke twice as much as Aminah whilst taking a similar number of turns. All the children asked a similar number of questions throughout the activity, while Habib and Samiha's mothers asked twice as many and Aminah's mother approximately three times more. It is interesting that the children asked more questions during the activities with their mothers than with their teachers. Also, the words-per-turn ratio increased with their mothers, as detailed in Table 5.2 (except with Aminah, whose ratio remained the same).

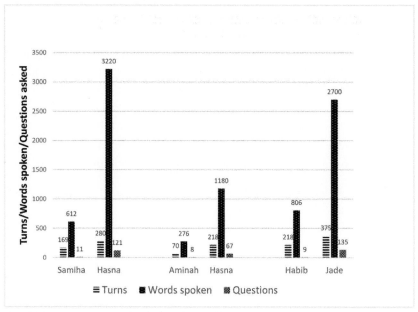

Participant	Number of Verbal Turns	Number of Words Spoken	Questions Asked by Each Participant
Samiha	169	612	11
Mother	280	3220	121
Aminah	70	276	8
Mother	218	1180	67
Habib	218	806	9
Mother	375	2700	135

Figure 5.1: Breakdown of the number of verbal turns, the number of words spoken, and the number of questions asked by each participant in the child–mother pairs

The relationships between the children and mothers in this study are complex. On the one hand, all the mothers have been raised by mothers who have strong faith and cultural backgrounds and, on the other hand, they have been through an education system similar to that of their children, thus sharing some of the experiences of their children's simultaneous worlds. Similar to the third-generation Bangladeshi children in Kenner *et al.*'s (2008) study, these children were also fluent English speakers, born and raised in the UK.

Table 5.2: Ratios of verbal turns, words per turn, words and questions asked in each child–mother pair

	Mother (Shamima) & Samiha	Mother (Layla) & Aminah	Mother (Thaminah) & Habib
Ratio of Turns Mother/Child	138/103 = 1.3	153/114 = 1.3	145/135 = 1.1
Ratio of Words Per Turn	Samiha: 568/103=5.5 Mother: 570/138=4	Aminah: 478/114=4.2 Mother: 1038/153=6.8	Habib: 876/135=6.5 Mother: 1091/145=7.5
Ratio of Words Mother/Child	570/568 = 1.0	1038/478 = 2.2	1091/876 = 1.2
Ratio of Questions Mother/Child	38/22 = 1.73	63/25 = 2.52	43/25 = 1.72

As we've seen, the language of communication between these children and their parents was mainly English. Tables 5.3 and 5.4 indicate interactions between the children and their mothers to be more equal than those with their teachers.

Table 5.3: Number of consecutive turns taken by the children and their mothers

Number of consecutive turns	2	3	4	5	6	7	8	9
Mother	28	6	1	2				
Samiha	19	7	3					
Mother	13	4	3					
Habib	21	9	1					
Mother	18	10	4	6		2		
Aminah	11	2	1					

Table 5.4 shows the breakdown of the types of questions asked by the children and their mothers during the activity.

Table 5.4: Child–mother pair: non-redundant, redundant, and self-responses

	Samiha	Mother (Shamima)	Aminah	Mother (Layla)	Habib	Mother (Thaminah)
No. of Non-Redundant Questions	10	19	20	31	17	34
No. of Redundant Questions	3	12	2	14	4	7
No. of Self-Response Questions	5	2	3	15	3	3
% of Redundant and Self-Response Questions	44%	42%	20%	48%	29%	23%

Although I expected Thaminah to be the most similar to the teachers, as she was a primary school teacher herself, it was in fact Layla who was. She had the highest percentage (48 per cent) of self-responses and redundant questions, and also asked the most questions (Figure 5.1). In the activity between Habib and his mother, Habib initiated the activity verbally (turns 1 and 2) and non-verbally (turns 5 and 7), which Thaminah endorsed (turn 3).

EXAMPLE 4 (child–mother pair: M: mother (Thaminah) and H: Habib)

1. ((H has the box and is looking at the picture on it))
2. H: eh it's a <u>solar system</u>
3. M: °solar system yeh°

Habib had the courage to disagree with his mother in the home setting (turn 27) and made suggestions (turns 44 and 50). The turns from 4–14 involved them both getting the pieces out of the box and turning pieces over. The moves 14–27 transcribed below are interesting, as they reflect a similar set of moves between Hasna and Samiha (Transcript Example 3, turns 6–9), where the child was being asked a very obvious question about the puzzle that was rhetorical.

14. ((H looks at a piece in his hands))
15. M: so how does the <u>puzzle</u> picture look <u>like</u>?
16. ((M looks down and continues turning over pieces))
17. H: looks like the solar <u>system</u>
18. ((H looks at M))
19. M: >oh ok then<
20. (...)
21. ((M laughs))
22. ((H smiles and slowly turns over the pieces))
23. M: >doesn't look like the solar system<
24. (..)
25. M: it looks like it's got <u>aliens</u> and
26. (2)
27. H: I don't think it's <u>aliens</u> because it looks like aliens but it's <u>actually astronauts</u>

They continued to discuss the planets and the solar system pieces between moves 28–41. Habib makes more decisive moves with his mother than he did with his teacher. When his mother suggested starting on a different part of the puzzle (turn 48), Habib made a confident move to continue with his attempt at making the part of the rocket (turn 50). They then continue putting pieces together between turns 51–397.

42. M: do you know anything about <u>space</u>?
43. ((GM talks to the toddler in Bengali in the background))
44. H: I'll make the rocket first let's make the rocket it's smaller
45. M: is it?
46. M: oh ok ( )
47. H: ok
48. M: Let's start with the aliens
49. ((H and M turn to look and face the box))
50. H: yeh you start with the <u>aliens</u> and I try [this the <u>rocket</u>]
51. M: [°here we are°]

The activity ends with Thaminah encouraging Habib to name all the planets, and they have a conversation about the solar system. The style of questioning was very similar to that of the teachers; the questions were direct and closed. However, with his mother, Habib seemed more at ease and ready to expand on his answers.

398. M: there done the solar system
399. H: that's the <u>whole solar system</u> with the <u>sun, Mercury</u> Venus uh uh
400. ((H swipes his hand over the completed puzzle))
401. ((Toddler is standing behind M and H observing them))
402. M: what is <u>that</u>?
403. ((M points to the planet Mercury))
404. H: Mercury
405. M: Mercury
406. H: yes   Earth,   Mars   Jup-Jupiter,   Saturn,   Neptune, U-Uranus, U-renus
407. ((Toddler sits on M's lap and observes))
408. M: °Uranus°
409. ((H points to puzzle))
410. H: Neptune then uh Pluto

In the activity between Aminah and her mother (Example 5), Aminah, like Habib, contributed more. Although her mother initiated the activity with a non-verbal move, Aminah made the first verbal move (turn 2). Layla seemed to take on Aminah's suggestions. However, she did take more consecutive turns, rather like the teachers. We see this in the short transcript below where Layla asked three consecutive questions (turns 8 and 9) with a directive non-verbal move (turn 15) that seemed to be intended to assess Aminah's knowledge. Aminah's responses to her mother were short, similar to those with her teacher.

EXAMPLE 5 (child–mother pair: M: mother (Layla) and A: Aminah)

1.   ((M takes out the puzzle pieces from the box and puts them on the floor; she checks to see if there are any more pieces left in the box, then puts the box to one side))
2.   A: put them the <u>right</u> way round
3.   M: ok let's do <u>ALL</u> of them then
4.   ((A and M start to turn over the pieces together in silence))
5.   ((M moves back a little to make space for more pieces))
6.   ((A spreads out some of the pieces behind her, turning to her side so she is facing all the pieces))
7.   (0.17)
8.   M: ok that's all spread out <u>now</u>
9.   ((A leans over towards mum))
10. (..)

11. M: <u>which</u> one shall we start with?
12. M: °is there any more in there?°
13. [((M picks up the box again and checks for any pieces left))]
14. [((A watches her))]
15. ((M then closes the box and holds it in front of her and A))
16. M: [it's gotta look like?]
17. (.)
18. ((M turns over the box in her hands, looking for the right picture to follow))
19. A: [°the man°]

Turns 20–81 continued, Layla asking many questions and Aminah responding, also asking a few herself. Although her contributions were brief, she responded more often as Layla asked for her contribution a lot more and at times followed some of it through. When they were stuck, Layla, like the teachers, suggested using the box as a guide, as can be seen in turn 82:

82. M: hmm let's have a look at the picture, oh you've got it and the next bit is the rocket shall we fit the rocket in there?

They worked more as partners in this activity than Aminah and her teacher and between turns 83–359 continued to find pieces and put them together. At the end of the task, Layla celebrated (turns 360–2) and, interestingly, Aminah demonstrated her confidence and took the role of establishing the learning outcome by putting herself forward to name all the planets to her mother (turn 364).

360. M: <u>hooray finished</u>!
361. (..)
362. M: *Masha Allah* **by Allah's Will** finished ok alright
363. ((M moves the box closer to herself and points at the completed puzzle))
364. A: shall I say all the names?
365. M: yeah
366. A: the solar system, Pluto, Mars, Jupiter what does that say?
367. M: Uranus

Transcript Example 6 is from the activity between Samiha and her mother. Here, again, it was the mother who started the activity by asking a question (turn 5), establishing who was the knowledgeable adult in the activity. Shamima also established the fact that Surayah, Samiha's younger sister, was there to help (turn 11), which was taken on board by Samiha (turn 12) and accepted with enthusiasm. Turns 1–9 were more teacher-like and this modelling of joint activity was interesting as Samiha later re-established her role as the knowledgeable one among the younger children. She took on the role of the teacher.

EXAMPLE 6 (child–mother pair: M: mother (Shamima), Ak: Akhter, Su: Surayah, and S: Samiha)

1. ((M and S are sitting opposite each other on the floor))
2. ((Su sitting next to M))
3. ((M holds the puzzle box and gets the pieces out))
4. ((S turns over the pieces of the puzzle))
5. M: what is it called?
6. ((M looks at the picture on the box))
7. ((S looks up))
8. S: ehm ehm jung – ehm ehm flo ehm jungle floor puzzle
9. M: jungle floor puzzle
10. (..)
11. M: yes Surayah is here to help
12. S: yep!
13. ((M continues to look at the box and places it on the floor, where S can see the large picture of the completed puzzle))
14. ((Ak is called away by his mother to the kitchen))
15. M: here is the picture

Interestingly, it is again the mother who suggested that the box be used as a guide (turn 15). Although Samiha seemed more relaxed with her mother than she was with her teacher, her mother tended to make more suggestions on how the pieces should be put together, taking on the role of the guide, as can be seen in turn 20 below:

20. M: ok shall I look for the green bits?
21. ((M points to the green parts on the box))

Also, in the portion of transcript below, the mother played a very teacher-like role in the way she suggested what pieces of the puzzle should be used. Even though Samiha made the suggestion (turn 29), her mother suggested starting with the sides and reinforced this in turn 34.

29. S: yeah! yeees! I think I've got something I think
30. ((S hands a piece of the puzzle to M))
31. (...)

32. M: I think we should start from the side
33. (…)
34. M: I found one side, I think it the pieces on that side

They continued to complete the puzzle, which Samiha took pride in achieving (turn 333), and her mother invited Surayah to join in and asked the children to evaluate the activity by naming all the animals in the puzzle and the noises they make (turn 343).

333. S: we done it!
334. ((M turns puzzle around to face the camera))
335. (..)
336. M: there you go!
337. ((S smiles))
338. (…)
339. M: Surayah?
340. ((M calls Su to have a look at the puzzle))
341. ((S holds out her hand to M to shake, which M does by holding out her hand, too))
342. ((Su looks at the puzzle))
343. M: talk about the picture to say what animals they are and what noises they make

In the child–mother pairs, the children contributed a lot more and seemed more relaxed than they did with their teachers. We saw in transcripts Example 4, 5, and 6 that the questions asked by the mothers were similar to those asked by the teachers, and the use of scaffolding apparent. All the mothers used words such as 'we' and 'let's', like the teachers, to indicate a sense of ownership and joint activity with the children.

The transcripts help to emphasize that even though the parents may be very teacher-like with their children at home, the conversations taking place were more dynamic, with the children contributing more and taking a little more ownership of the activity. Their voices were heard a little more than when they were with their teachers. Tizard and Hughes (2002) found that although nursery staff spent a great deal of time talking to children, their conversations were infrequent and often restricted to a few brief exchanges compared to those taking place at home. The mothers differed from the teachers in the way they scaffolded and guided the children's input, possibly due to the context of the home being away from the formal setting of the school. All the children demonstrated their 'learner flexibilities' by being able to adapt their practices to suit the context in which they were interacting. Although the teachers and mothers were dominating the talk, the conversation did not become a monologue; the children kept up their end of the conversations making responses and contributions when required or encouraged. They contributed to the collaborative enterprise: without these minimal but appropriate responses from the children, the teachers and mothers would not have felt able to play their part. Learner flexibility is further demonstrated in the next chapter, where we see the children completing the activities with their grandmothers.

Chapter 6

Exploring intergenerational learning between children and their grandmothers

Alongside the benefits teachers can gain from drawing on children's funds of knowledge and involving parents, Al-Azami (2006) and Kenner *et al.* (2004, 2007) suggest intergenerational learning with grandparents has potential advantages for all three parties: pupils, grandparents, and schools. For pupils, there is learning in an enjoyable and relaxed manner while also building on a 'special relationship': 'It was fun learning with grandma because we do everything together' (Gyllenspetz, 2007: 26). For grandparents, recognition of a 'teaching' role and involvement in their grandchild's learning was associated with feelings of increased self-worth: 'It was lovely to feel involved in my grandchild's education'; 'I feel more confident in helping with reading and writing' (Gyllenspetz, 2007: 21).

These positive learning outcomes were achieved through a 'special relationship' that is found to exist between the two generations (Al-Azami, 2006). One reason for this could be that the older generation are less involved in the everyday world and have less responsibility and therefore potentially have more free time to focus on grandchildren. In general, grandparents' relationships with grandchildren are a positive and satisfying experience for grandparents (Drew, 2000). Drew reviewed research on grandparenthood and found that, through interaction, grandparents had significant influence on the development of their grandchildren. This influence becomes particularly interesting when investigating how cultures evolve as communities of people move from their country of origin to join another host community, as is the case with the families in this book.

This chapter captures the communicative purposes and functions of the grandmothers' and children's actions in relation to one another, in contrast to those within the child–teacher and child–mother pairs, addressing the following aspects:

- patterns of interaction
- language use
- talk and the nature of partnership
- the child as teacher.

Through the above analysis, we can see how the following concepts from sociocultural theory apply to the intergenerational learning encounters: guided participation, scaffolding, synergy leading to mutual benefits for the young children and the adults, 'syncretizing' knowledge from different sources, funds of knowledge within communities, and the transmission of knowledge, or prolepsis, between generations.

Patterns of interaction

Samiha and her grandmother sat together on the living room floor of Samiha's maternal aunt's house with their family all around them. Aminah and her grandmother, Panna, were in the grandmother's house in a little bedroom on the second floor sitting on the bed, not the floor, as Panna had back problems. The bed was quite soft and the puzzle pieces were difficult to put together. Panna sat on one corner of the bed and Aminah sat facing the room on the side of the bed with her back to the window. Habib and his grandmother sat next to each other on the floor of Habib's aunt's room. Habib's and Aminah's mothers both said that it would disturb the activity if they were to stay in the room. The details of the puzzles and the length of time taken to complete is in Table 6.1 below:

Table 6.1: Record of puzzles and times taken to complete them by each child–grandmother pair

	Aminah & Grandmother (Panna)	Samiha & Grandmother (Rekha)	Habib & Grandmother (Rahma)
Name of Puzzle	Jungle Floor Puzzle	Jungle Floor Puzzle	Jungle Floor Puzzle
No. of Pieces	24-piece puzzle featuring a cartoon jungle scene with lots of creatures	24-piece puzzle featuring a cartoon jungle scene with lots of creatures	24-piece puzzle featuring a cartoon jungle scene with lots of creatures
Time Taken	13:58	11:36	08:28
Total No. of Turns (Verbal & Non-Verbal)	369	385	268

All the grandmothers completed the Jungle Floor puzzle with their grandchildren. As the puzzle contained fewer and larger pieces than the other two, the activity took less time to complete. Therefore, significantly fewer turns were taken and fewer words spoken. However, the patterns for the child–grandmother pairs were similar in many ways to the child–mother pairs. Here, too, from Figure 6.1 above we see that the ratios of turns were more equal between the participants. All the grandmothers asked twice as many questions as their grandchildren. The ratio of words per turn between each child and their grandmother (Table 6.2) was also fairly similar except in Habib's case. Habib uttered twice as many words as his grandmother. Although Samiha had completed this puzzle with her mother, she repeated the same one with her grandmother because I wanted to observe all the children carrying out the same puzzle with their grandmothers. This did not impact too greatly on the way Samiha interacted with her grandmother, as the time lapse between the activities was approximately a year.

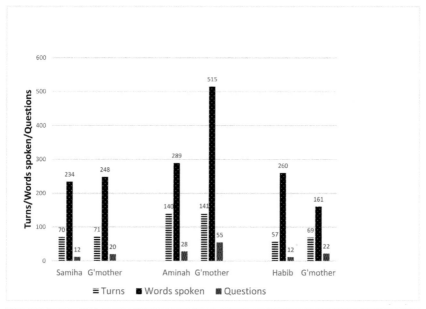

Participant	Number of Verbal Turns	Number of Words Spoken	Questions Asked by Each Participant
Samiha	70	234	12
Grandmother	71	248	20
Aminah	140	289	28
Grandmother	141	515	55
Habib	57	260	12
Grandmother	69	161	22

Figure 6.1: Breakdown of the number of verbal turns, the number of words spoken, and the number of questions asked by each participant in the child–grandmother pairs

Table 6.2: Ratios of verbal turns, words per turn, words and questions asked in each child–grandmother pair

	Samiha & Grandmother (Panna)	Aminah & Grandmother (Layla)	Habib & Grandmother (Shamima)
Ratio of Turns	71/70 = 1.0	141/140 = 1.0	69/57 = 1.2
Ratio of Words Per Turn	Samiha: 234/70=3.3 Grandmother: 248/71=3.5	Aminah: 289/140=2.1 Grandmother: 515/141=3.7	Habib: 260/57=4.7 Grandmother: 161/69=2.3
Ratio of Words Grandmother/ Child	248/234 = 1.1	515/289 = 1.8	161/260 = 0.6
Ratio of Questions Grandmother/ Child	20/12 = 1.7	55/28 = 2.0	22/12 = 1.8

The relationships between the children and their grandmothers were similar to the relationships with their mothers, but very different to those with their teachers. To delve into this a little further, I explored the interactional components during the activities by looking at the nature of the following:

- turn-taking
- exchange pairs – question-and-answer patterns

Turn-taking Patterns

> When a child makes or fails to make a particular kind of utterance, consider characteristics of the situation as well as of the child.
>
> Cazden, 1971: 48

Following Cazden, the data and findings presented in this section demonstrate how each child responded to their different contexts, how they found their way through the shared activities, and the choices they made regarding the roles they chose for themselves. They used particular strategies and adapted their roles depending on which adult they were interacting with. The children did not always make their choice of role consciously: sometimes they were determined by the constraints imposed on them by the adults and the boundaries set by the context they were in. Although the situations were very similar and the children employed some of the same strategies, each child used the resources at their disposal, demonstrating their ability to adapt and their 'learner flexibility'.

In the child–grandmother pairs, the turn-taking patterns were reversed. We see the infrequency of the grandmothers' turns and the frequency with which the children take the initiative, assuming the role of the more experienced person. They asked questions as well as answered them, sometimes taking the lead in moving from one topic to another. They could respond to their grandmothers and take heed of their contributions and those of the other children present. This can be seen in the example of Samiha during her activities with both her mother and grandmother. The children were confident and showed that they were receptive and able to build on prior skills and knowledge from their different and sometimes 'simultaneous worlds'.

The children were most relaxed with their grandmothers. Tables 6.3 and 6.4 illustrate the greater equality between the number of consecutive turns taken by the children and by their grandmothers. Even though the grandmothers seemed to ask more non-redundant questions, the percentage of redundant and self-response questions was lower than those between the child–mother and child–teacher pairs, indicating an increase in the interaction between them. According to the questionnaire data, these grandmothers engaged in a lot of activities with their grandchildren, such as reading, memorizing, gardening, and many others, similar to the grandparents in the study by Kenner *et al.* (2004b). So we know they were creating joint interactions where learning encounters took place.

Table 6.3: Number of consecutive turns taken by each child and their grandmother

Number of consecutive turns	2	3	4	5	6	7	8	9
Grandmother	6	2	1					
Samiha	9	1	1					
Grandmother	9	1						
Habib	3	3	1					1
Grandmother	14	3	1					
Aminah	14	3		1				

Table 6.4 shows a breakdown of the types of questions asked by the children and their grandmothers during the activity.

Table 6.4: Child–grandmother pair: non-redundant, redundant, and self-responses

	Samiha	Grand-mother (Rekha)	Aminah	Grand-mother (Panna)	Habib	Grand-mother (Rahma)
No. of Non-Redundant Questions	7	11	19	37	8	18
No. of Redundant Questions	2	6	1	11	3	3
No. of Self-Response Questions			3	5		
% of Redundant and Self-Response Questions	22%	35%	17%	30%	27%	14%

In the transcripts below it is evident that the children assumed the role of the more knowledgeable person when it came to putting the puzzle together. It is also clear that the turns were not allocated by a single director, but rather seemed to be negotiated as the talk proceeded. Aminah's grandmother, Panna, was the most fluent in English of the grandmothers. Her interaction with Aminah was interesting as Aminah, although still shy, interacted much more with her grandmother than she did with her mother or teacher. Here (Example 7), Aminah initiated the activity (turn 1), introducing the puzzle to her grandmother, who positively reinforced this by saying that it's a '*shundor* puzzle **nice** puzzle' (turn 3), supported by her non-verbal move (turn 4) showing interest in the picture on the box. This also put Aminah at ease and aided in setting up a relaxed approach to the task. Aminah agreed and pondered upon what the next move should be (turns 5 and 6).

EXAMPLE 7 (Aminah–grandmother pair: GM: grandmother (Panna), and A: Aminah)

1. A: ahh this is a <u>JUNGLE</u> puzzle
2. ((A takes out pieces of the puzzle and puts them on the bed))

3. GM: *shundor* puzzle **nice** puzzle
4. ((GM leans forward to look at the picture on the box))
5. A: °hmm°
6. (0.5)

The following sequence, made up of turns 7–13, gives an indication of the way the verbal and non-verbal moves made by Aminah and Panna were complementary. The sequence begins with a directive from grandmother Panna, which was followed up by a supportive non-verbal move (turn 8), making space for Aminah to carry out the action (turn 10). This sequence shows how they worked together, the grandmother playing the role of the facilitator.

7. GM: *shokholti baar khori lou* **get all the pieces out**
8. ((GM moves a few pieces away to make space))
9. (0.11)
10. ((A leans forward on her knees and takes the rest of the pieces out of the box))
11. ((GM moves pieces away))
12. ((After A finishes, she puts the box to one side))
13. A: ( )

In the next sequence of turns (14–20), the verbal initiating move (turn 14) made by the grandmother was followed by a subtle non-verbal supportive move (turn 15). By scratching her chin, she indicated to Aminah that there was room for suggestions. This, along with turn 17, allowed Aminah to come up with some complex turns (16 and 18). In this section of the interaction it was interesting how Panna allowed or scaffolded Aminah's learning to play the role of the teacher through her gentle and supportive approach.

14. GM: *ono ano* **here here**
15. ((GM points to the box and scratches her chin))
16. A: let's separate them
17. GM: hmm
18. A: so we can see the picture, we need to keep this so we can keep it right over there
19. ((A picks up the box and props it up against the foot of the bed))
20. (..)

The grandmother's facilitative role continued into the next sequence of turns (21–26) where she initiated the sequence with a directive (turn 21)

followed by a whisper. Similar to turn 15 above, this also worked to prompt
Aminah to assume the role of teacher, which she did by asking a teacher-like
question (turn 23). Here, again, she was supported by her grandmother's
gentle 'hmm' (turn 25). It was an interesting combination of turns where,
once again, the grandmother initiated the turn (turn 21) and supported
Aminah, allowing her to feel in control of the situation and make some
complex suggestions. The synergy in their interaction was visible through
the supportive and compatible turns taken between them, enabling them to
complete the activity.

21. GM: corner *bhar khoro* **take out** corner we need the corner
22. ((GM whispers something))
23. A: ok shall we start from the edges?
24. ((A sits back looks at GM))
25. GM: °hmm°
26. A: ok [one edge] ( )

Towards the end of the activity, Aminah did not resist handing the role of
expert over to her grandmother and Panna took on the role in a smooth
transition (turns 245 and 246) by asking Aminah to observe what they
had put together. Panna spoke mostly English when they were putting the
puzzle together but after the task was completed and she took the lead in
the discussion, she spoke more Bengali with Aminah as we see below.

245. GM: *shesh ni ekhon?* **is it finished now?**
246. GM: *eta khita oilo dekho sain* **what is it have a look**
247. A: jungle
248. GM: jungle picture *dekhao amare* **show me**
249. ((A picks up box and shows GM))
250. A: it's this
251. GM: picture'*e khita khita amere dekho sain* **show me what things are there in the** picture
252. A: hmm?
253. GM: *khita ase* picture'*o* **what is in the** picture?
254. ((A points to each animal in the picture as she says the names))
255. A: *eta* **this is** frog
256. GM: hmm

Aminah responded to her grandmother's gentle but persistent probing.
She named the animals in English and her grandmother acknowledged her
input with 'hmm's. This trend continued between turns 257–75. Panna then

introduced Bengali into the interaction by asking Aminah to say 'crocodile' in Bengali (turn 277). Aminah did not hesitate to throw the question back at Panna (turn 278), demonstrating the relaxed learning environment created by Panna where Aminah could be confident in the interaction. From this point onward the pattern continued with Panna naming the animals in Bengali and Aminah repeating after her.

276. A: and waterfall
277. GM: crocodile*'re khita khoi Banglath?* **how do you say crocodile in Bangla?**
278. A: *khita?* **what?**
279. GM: *kumeer*
280. A: hmm
281. GM: *eta khita?* **what's that?**
282. A: eta baby <u>monkey</u>
283. GM: *eta banor Banglath* **it's** *banor* **in Bangla**
284. A: *banor*

In the next series of turns Panna helped Aminah to reflect on her visits to Bangladesh by talking about the puzzle. Although Aminah took brief turns, thanks to Panna's thoughtful questioning, she was enabled to extend her knowledge by visualizing the context in which she could use and practise her Bengali.

313. GM: hmm *ota dekhsoni gaas?* **did you see those trees?**
314. A: *gaas* **trees**
315. GM: *khono aasil?* **where were they?**
316. A: Bangladesh
317. GM: Bangladesh *amrar goror shamne ni* **in front of our house?**
318. A: yes
319. GM: *ar ekhano khita khelaisilai?* **and what did you play there?**
320. GM: Badminton
321. A: *na* **no**
322. GM: *ammu khelaisilo ni?* **did mum play?**
323. A: *ami zani na* **I don't know**
324. GM: yes *tumi buli gesso tumi soto asilai tho* **you forgot you were little that's why**

Similarly, in turns 345–58 below, repetitive prompts from her grandmother gave Aminah the confidence to share experiences of where she had seen the animals in her context in the UK. As Panna responded with the supportive 'hmm's, Aminah expanded her responses and contributed longer turns.

345. GM: hmm yes *ar khita dekhsilai?* **what else did you see?**
346. GM: fish
347. A: fish
348. GM: hmm
349. A: and nowadays only we can see in the jungle lions and monkeys
350. GM: hmm hmm
351. A: I suppose in some [countries]
352. GM: [and those] birds you can see in the jungle and not in the countryside
353. A: yes and in the zoo you can see lions
354. GM: hmm
355. A: in the aquariums you can see <u>hippos</u>
356. GM: hmm
357. (..)
358. A: then in pet shops you can see parrots

In the activity between Samiha and her grandmother, Example 8, as when she pursued the activity with her mother, her younger siblings and cousin joined in. Samiha was at ease with the camera being focused on them, entering her role naturally. Below we see Samiha comfortable and enthusiastic in the interaction with her grandmother. Rekha initiated 'playing with language' (Drury, 2003) as a key strategy for learning Bengali and building rapport. The activity began with the grandmother taking the initiative by removing all the pieces from the box. Samiha started the activity using Bengali and Rekha started the verbal turns with a slight, playful challenge (turn 5).

EXAMPLE 8 (Samiha–grandmother pair: GM: grandmother (Rekha), Su: Surayah, M: mother (Shamima), and S: Samiha)

1. ((Toddler sitting on mum's lap on sofa, observing the action on the floor))
2. ((GM takes all the pieces of the puzzle out of the box))
3. ((Su sits a little distance away from GM and S on GM's right, and starts to play with a couple of pieces))
4. S: (Bengali)
5. GM: ( ) *sinona kheltao sinona* **don't know how to play**

6. ((S takes the box from GM's hand and moves the box to the front, so they can see the picture of the whole puzzle on the box))
7. S: *okhta dekhtai bade* **you need to look at that later**
8. ((S and Su lean forward, and GM looks at the box))
9. ((S points at the picture))
10. GM: *khonta dekhtai?* **look at which one**
11. S: *okhta dekhtai ola banaitai* **look at that and make it like that**
12. ((S puts the box away besides her and starts to separate the pieces))
13. M: picture
14. S: hmm
15. ((S moves the box again a little further away))

In this sequence of turns, Samiha tried to convince Rekha to use the puzzle box as a guide, just as all the teachers had done. The teachers initiated using the picture on the puzzle's box to help with putting the puzzle together. The mothers also used the box to guide their activity. However, in the child–grandmother pairs the roles were reversed. The children took the lead in using the box as a guide, as shown above. Samiha's mother emphasized this to support her (turn 13). Although Rekha entertained the idea of the box, she had her own approach, which she initiated in turn 16, encouraging Samiha to think for herself and find a starting point. The mother's role here did not change much from the role she played when carrying out the activity with Samiha. We see in turn 13 above that she was still directive in her approach, but here, in turn 16, she uses more Bengali, although this was directed at Rekha, not Samiha. Samiha took on the directive tone like her mother and teacher (turns 18 and 20).

16. GM: *khita banaitai kholla bhar khoro* **what do you want to make find the head**
17. ((GM holds a piece in her hand))
18. S: *tumi oooh tumi eta khoro* **you oooh you do that one**
19. (..)
20. S: *ar* tidy *khoro* **and** tidy **up**
21. GM: *dekhi dekhi ubau* **let's see let's see wait**
22. M: sky *khoro phoila* **do the** sky **first**
23. S: *ami* sky *khorram* hmm **I am doing the** sky **hmm**
24. M: *tumi otha horraia* **you move those** turn it all around
25. ((S leans over to turn some pieces over))

26. ((Su watches S))
27. ((GM tries to put a couple of pieces together))
28. ((Su joins in turning over pieces))

Drury (2003) points to having fun with language as an important strategy for developing language competence. This is true for Samiha. In the following extract, after the puzzle was complete, Rekha, like Panna, assumed the role of expert by asking Samiha to reflect on their accomplishment of the puzzle (turn 317). Rekha initiated the sequence of turns by asking a question to which she knew the answer in Bengali, but she didn't know which language would be used in response. Thus it was a genuine question – to which Samiha responded in English but fluently inserted Bengali words. The mother addressed Rekha in Bengali, encouraging her to answer Samiha (turn 321). Here the grandmother took two consecutive turns (322 and 323), possibly to encourage Samiha to interact in Bengali. However, the mother again tried to direct Rekha, this time to use English (turn 324), which is immediately taken up by Samiha. To ease Rekha into this, Samiha whispers into her grandmother's ear and smiles, and Rekha amuses them by saying 'hmm frog *hoise ni* **is it right?**'

317. GM: *eta khita oise?* **what is that?**
318. ((GM points to the complete puzzle))
319. S: parrot, snake I don't know what that is *eta khita?* **what's that?**
320. ((S looks at GM))
321. M: *amma khou* the **mum say** the
322. GM: *eta khita?* **what's that?**
323. GM: *Baag beng* **tiger frog**
324. M: English'*e khou the* **say it in** English **then**
325. S: frog frog frog
326. ((S whispers in GM's ear and smiles))
327. GM: hmm frog *hoise ni?* **is it right?**
328. S: hippopotamus
329. ((S says with an accent))
330. ((GM leans forward and presses the pieces on))
331. ((Su copies GM and does the same))

This banter continues for a while, and from the extract below, with the encouragement from her grandmother, Samiha was no longer using self-assertion; instead, there was genuine language play on a mutual level using both Bengali and English.

361. GM: *tomar ta urer na amar ta urer* **your one is not flying my one is flying**
362. ((GM looks at S and Su, and puts out her hands to make a flying gesture))
363. S: ehm *ochta taile amar uphre urer!* ehm **that one is mine and is flying high!**
364. ((S points to a bird in flight))
365. GM: *ochta kala!* **that is black!**
366. ((S smirks and they look at each other))
367. ((S puts her arms up in frustration))
368. S: hmm! so *amar* beak *kala tomar lal ar* green *ar* white hmm! So **my** beak **is black yours is** green **and** white
369. ((S makes gestures with her hands))
370. GM: *amar dekho* green *ase*, red *ase*, *tia rong o ase*, orange *ase* **look I have** green, **have** red, **also have turquoise, have** orange
371. ((GM leans forward and points to the picture while stating all the colours))
372. ((S makes head movements in rhythm with GM's tone))

Rekha 'orchestrated' (Ruby *et al.*, 2010) the activity so all could play their part in getting the puzzle done. She used strategies that allowed each participant to feel as though they were an important part of the process. Firstly, she was inclusive in her approach, which included the mother, Samiha, and Surayah all taking part in different capacities. The whole activity began with the toddler observing the participants and Surayah observing and copying some of the actions (turns 331 and 362). Samiha's mother took part without hesitation, and Rekha, as we have seen above, complied with her request to interact in English. Her interaction with Samiha was collaborative and they learned from each other bringing forth their strengths to accomplish the activity. They used the opportunity to learn and build their knowledge base of Bengali and English as well as refining the technical knowledge required to put the puzzle together through mutually guided participation, so allowing synergy in their interaction. The perfect end to the activity was shaped by the grandmother: she pointed out their equal partnership by saying '*amar ar tomar* mine and yours' (turn 385).

380. S: *tumi khoiso ochta tomar ar shobta amar* **you said that is yours and the rest is mine**
381. ((S tries to push GM's hand out of the way))
382. GM: everything *amar* **mine**

383. S: everything *amar* **mine**
384. ((S mimics GM's accent and tone, and they look at each other))
385. GM: *amar ar tomar* **mine and yours**

Of the three grandmothers, Rahma was the most fragile as she had been unwell before the videoing took place. In the activity between Habib and his grandmother (Example 9), he made certain choices during the interaction. He decided when it was acceptable for him to carry out the action of putting the pieces together by himself and the times he needed to involve his grandmother by giving her instructions that she would understand and follow. Turns 2–12 were all carried out without either of them speaking a word. Neither seemed uneasy spending that time trying to sort out the pieces and the grandmother trying to put pieces together. We see below how Habib took the lead, guiding his grandmother through the activity.

EXAMPLE 9 (Habib–grandmother pair: GM: grandmother (Rahma), and H: Habib)

1. (0.56)
2. ((H and GM are sitting next to each other on the floor))
---
10. ((GM is trying to put pieces together))
11. ((H spreads out the pieces of the puzzle in front of them))
12. ((GM sits back and watches H spread the pieces out))

Habib was clearly in the role of teacher using a lot of directives in the exchanges with his grandmother. Much of his language use related to the language used by teachers and mothers, as most of the verbal turns he took reflected the language of instruction. Habib gave his grandmother a series of instructions backed up by supportive non-verbal moves (turns 16–18). He tried to assist her subtly by putting the box in front of them both as a guide. The grandmother participated actively as she tried to put pieces together, responding to his directives but allowing her grandson to take the lead. Her simple 'hmm's indicated to him her involvement and acceptance of his role.

13. H: °*ota okhano zai*° °**that goes here**°
14. (0.6)
15. ((GM takes the two pieces from H and attaches them to her pieces))
16. ((H sits back and watches her))

17. ((H moves the box from next to him and places it in front of them both))
18. ((H leans forward to help GM put the pieces on properly))
19. H: *[ochta]* [that]
20. GM: °[hmm]°
21. H: >*okhano zai na*< >doesn't go there<
22. GM: °hmm°

Their interaction became more collaborative as they progressed. Habib managed to scaffold his grandmother's learning, as can be seen, to the point where it develops into a partnership.

111. GM: °hmm *ono* <u>*ono*</u> *tomar khore di*° °there <u>there</u> behind you°
112. H: *oino ochta* <u>*okhano zai*</u> that one does <u>go there</u>
113. GM: °*hoise*° °that's it°
114. H: *ar* <u>*ochta*</u> °*okhano zai*° and <u>that</u> °one goes there°

Like the other grandmothers, Rahma assumed the role of the expert after the puzzle was complete. She made considerable use of contextual clues and had knowledge of Habib's experiences of life in the UK and visits to Bangladesh. Rahma could guess what the child would learn from discussing their shared experience of visits to Bangladesh. She helped him build a conversation, using Bengali, about a topic that was clearly of interest to them. In their turns, Rahma encouraged Habib to extend the topic by contributing to the discussion (turns 214 and 216). And she took his contributions further in simple and related moves, which enabled him to explore and express more fully the topic under discussion. By giving Habib more information, she enabled him to extend both his language use and their knowledge of the topic. This was evident in the ways Rahma modified her utterances so that Habib could make sense of them. She kept them short and simple, enabling him to take longer and more complex turns (213 and 218).

210. GM: *beng beng* frog frog
211. H: *eeeh dekhsilam tura* yes saw little
212. GM: hmm
213. H: *amrar barir sham-<u>khore</u> okhano* pond *asil* there was a pond <u>behind</u> our village
214. GM: pond *asil [thahole tho beng asil]* there was a pond [then there were frogs]
215. H: *[khali amra dekhsilam]* [only we saw them]
216. GM: *beng asilo bandor nai* there were frogs and no monkeys

217. ((H and GM look down at the puzzle))
218. H: *na amra* jungle'*o gesilam na* but waterfall *amra zaitam asilam* and photo *dekhsilam* ehm dark colour *phore ekhta* waterfall *amrar desho* <u>no</u> **we didn't go to the** jungle but **were supposed to go to the** waterfall and **saw** photo ehm **there was** dark colour **and a** waterfall **in our country**
219. ((H and GM look at each other, then down at the puzzle))
220. ((H traces the water with his left hand))

While the grandmother's presence was visible during all three pairs' activities, many of the moves that the teachers normally monopolize were clearly being taken by the children, such as asking direct questions and giving instructions. Although with the child–grandmother pairs roles were reversed, with the children being the expert, the grandmothers took over the role once the puzzle was completed, by discussing the puzzle in both Bengali and English. They contextualized that knowledge. For example, Panna and Rahma probed Aminah and Habib to think back to their visits to Bangladesh sharing their own experiences, giving rise to prolepsis where knowledge is transmitted from one generation to another. The interactions between the children and their grandmothers involved synergy through mutual sharing of knowledge and guided participation. The children's ability to exercise their learner flexibilities enabled grandmothers and grandchildren each to support the other's needs, thus establishing a relationship that Kenner *et al.* (2007) characterize as one of 'mutuality'. Also, like siblings, the grandmothers were essential mediating agents (Kelly, 2004) between languages and cultural experiences, rousing the children's interest, developing their understanding of Bengali and expanding their knowledge base about the topic.

Language use

> If the language environment is natural, consistent and stimulating, children will pick up whatever languages are around.
> Crystal, 1987, cited in Brown, 2009: 160

So far it is clear that the children play a critical role in taking control of their own learning through utilizing the opportunities provided to them by the adults involved. The way Bengali and English were used changed the nature of the interaction and the role the child played with each adult. As the teacher's manner of speaking was in many ways similar to the mother's and different to the grandmother's, the children responded differently to them, able to adapt. So they demonstrated competences and flexibilities with their mothers and grandmothers that were not visible or known to their teachers.

One of the features of all the child–teacher interactions was that all communication was in English. This was even the case with Hasna and the two children who were, like her, bilingual in English and Bengali. This was also true of the mothers: all three conversed with their children in English throughout the activities, even though all were fluent speakers of Bengali and English. However, the mothers of both Habib and Samiha switched to Bengali when addressing the younger siblings. Samiha was the only child who spoke Bengali during the activity with her mother, but only to speak to her little sister, Surayah:

EXAMPLE 10 (M: mother; S: Samiha and Su: Surayah)

> 344. M: what pieces have you got?
> 345. M: Oooh
> 346. ((M tries to prise it from Su))
> 347. (…)
> 348. ((Su leans towards S))
> 349. S: *dilou dilou dilou* **give give give**
> 350. ((S says in a coaxing voice))

During this extract, Samiha and her mother were both putting pieces together. Her mother then turned to Surayah to see what pieces she had in her hands. She tried to take the piece from Surayah but Surayah leaned towards Samiha. Samiha responded to the situation by asking Surayah to hand over the puzzle piece. Although their mother spoke to Surayah in English at first, as the activity progressed both Samiha and her mother code-switched between Bengali and English with Surayah. Habib's mother did the same when she was speaking to Maryam, Habib's younger sister, although only once. Maryam sat to the side with her grandmother while Habib and his mother completed the puzzle. Towards the end, Maryam came near, hovered around them and observed them. She also started to whine a little as she was tired, and her mother responded to her:

EXAMPLE 11 (M: mother)

> 370. M: Maryam *khita khor rai?* Maryam **what are you doing?**
> 371. M: coat *zaitaigni ni?* coat **do you want to go?**

Habib's grandmother was sitting in the same room but away from the activity when he and his mother were completing the puzzle. The only times (turns 174 and 178) she spoke Bengali during the activity was when she tried to help him find a piece he was searching for:

EXAMPLE 12 (H: Habib; GM: grandmother; and M: mother)

> 173. H: right there's <u>one part left</u>
> 174. GM: *tomar khore di ase dekho* **it's behind you look**
> 175. ((GM speaks from the background))
> 176. ((H and M turn to look at GM))
> 177. (...)
> 178. GM: *oi dekho tomar khore di* **there look it's behind you**
> 179. H: <u>yep</u> this is what I need ehm <u>this part's</u> at the long
> 180. ((H finds pieces behind him))

While Aminah and her mother did the activity, Aminah only responded once to her mother in Bengali, towards the end of their shared activity, dictating where Aminah should put the piece of puzzle by saying '*acha* ok' (turn 329). All three children addressed their mothers as *ammu* or *amma*, which is a Bengali term of endearment. There are other terms that Samiha's mother encouraged, such as *apu* and *bhaiaa,* which are used to address older siblings, and *nanu* for grandmother. The most marked difference in the use of Bengali took place during the child–grandmother pairs, where the participants' interaction in Bengali increased considerably, as can be seen in Table 6.5.

Table 6.5: Number of words spoken in Bengali and English by the children with their grandmothers

	Aminah	Grand-mother (Panna)	Samiha	Grand-mother (Rekha)	Habib	Grand-mother (Rahma)
No. of Words Spoken in English	312	258	112	8	37	12
No. of Words Spoken in Bengali	70	230	136	241	168	134

For both Samiha and Habib, Bengali was used from the beginning of the activity, as they initiated the first verbal interactional turn of the activity in Bengali. For Aminah it took a little longer before her grandmother managed to coax her into using Bengali. Although Aminah initiated the activity in English, her grandmother responded in Bengali. Her grandmother code-switched between Bengali and English until, in turn 65, Aminah responded to herself (turn 63) in Bengali:

EXAMPLE 13 (A: Aminah)

63. A: and <u>this</u> might go <u>here</u>
64. (..)
65. A: *na zanin na* yes ... *eta?* **no don't know** yes ... **this?**

Interestingly, Aminah's grandmother did not pressure Aminah to use English or Bengali and eased her in by using the pause fillers, 'hmm', which encouraged Aminah to code-switch between Bengali and English.

Although the children's command of Bengali was weaker than their command of English, they still managed to keep up the conversation using both languages to complete the activity. Because their grandmothers were not fluent in English, Habib and Samiha persevered, thus speaking very little English during the activity. Most of Samiha's use of English was directed at her mother and younger sister and she conversed with her grandmother almost entirely in Bengali. Evidently, according to the table, Habib actually spoke more words in Bengali than his grandmother.

After the activities, I noted that in their extended conversations with their grandmothers the children were more discursive or exploratory than when talking with their mothers and teachers. The grandmothers recalled past events, discussed what the children had seen on their visits to Bangladesh, or encouraged the children to learn the names and colours of the animals in the puzzle. The concluding conversations were facilitated by the grandmothers freeing the children's attention from the pressure of action (getting the puzzle done) so they could attempt to achieve mutual understanding. Even though the children had restricted powers of expression in Bengali, they managed to keep up the conversations with their grandmothers, and the grandmothers in turn made the effort to understand the child's intended meaning and to extend it in terms the child could understand. This required them to be willing to listen, which was characterized often by the 'hmm's and pauses. The grandmothers had the ability to pitch what they said at the right level by using simple and accessible Bengali and keeping the utterances in the turns brief. The way the children and their grandmothers interacted with one another – code-switching and engaging in mutual sharing of expertise, but also bringing the learning to a meaningful level by contextualizing it with regard to their experiences – demonstrates the level of syncretic learning involved during the shared endeavours.

Talk and the nature of partnership

> The process of learning how to negotiate communicatively is the very process by which one enters the culture.
>
> Bruner, 1984, cited in Edwards and Westgate, 1987: 12

When a conversation is between two participants who are unequally matched, such as between an adult and a child, the expectation is that the adult will be the knowledgeable participant. This places great responsibility on the adult to compensate for the child's limitations and to behave in ways that make it as easy as possible for the child to play their part effectively. As with all scaffolding, once the purpose for which it is erected has been achieved and the child is able to play their part in the conversation, it is gradually dismantled. This partnership is very evident between the children and their teachers and parents.

The nature of talk with the teachers was fast-paced and the teachers attempted to complete the activity as quickly as possible. The partnership between the child–teacher pair was one in which each would support the other to get the task done with the teacher as the guide. This involved finding a strategy and a plan, as seen in the extracts below:

HASNA AND AMINAH

    16. H: do you want to tell me what to do first?

    22. H: do you know how best to do a <u>jigsaw</u>?

HASNA AND SAMIHA

    25. H: >gosh we're in the same boat, so I know what why don't you think of a strategy?<

JADE AND HABIB

    56. Jade: ok what's our plan to go first?

    57. Jade: to do what are we looking for first?

The roles the children took when they encountered difficulties in the activities were interesting. The teachers were first to express themselves verbally, as in the following extracts:

HASNA AND AMINAH

224. H: oh yes ( ) oh look we're not °getting far at all°
225. ((A sits and watches))
226. ((H tries to put pieces together))
227. (0.7)
228. A: °maybe we should° ( )
229. ((A holds a couple of pieces, then stands up and leans over the pieces near H))

JADE AND HABIB

186. J: aahh it's <u>quite hard isn't it</u>?
187. ((H nods yes))
188. J: do you think there's any <u>other BITS</u> that go <u>together</u>?
189. J: maybe we could look at those before and then when we're looking >maybe we can just find by <u>accident</u> that piece< °we got loads of pieces on that one°
190. ((H continues looking for pieces))

HASNA AND SAMIHA

134. H: do you know what?
135. H: I feel like <u>giving up</u> already <u>how do you feel</u>?
136. ((H laughs))
137. S: °not really [because]°
138. H: [very] good at this then let's stick with it for a bit
139. S: °where that goes?°
140. ((S looks at H))

The children all persevered with the task throughout, and Samiha said confidently that she didn't find it difficult (turn 137). When she tried to elaborate, she was interrupted by Hasna (turn 138). Such interruptions did not occur with the mothers or grandmothers. On the contrary, each participant in the child–grandmother pairs boosted the other's confidence by encouraging them to continue when they felt there was a difficult bit. Panna says to Aminah '*tumi zano na ni?* **don't** you **know**?' and '*Zanbai* you **will know where this one go?**' (turns 158 and 159). When Rekha asked Samiha, '*tomar piece phailaiso ar amar khoi phaitam khoi thaki?* **you found your piece and where shall I find my piece where?**', Samiha encouraged her grandmother to look, and once Rekha accomplished fitting her pieces, she reassured Samiha by saying, 'hmm *sintha khorio na* hmm **don't worry**'. The partnership here was meaningful, encouraging, and mutually supportive. The children and their grandmothers communicated with each other well, and the roles they played were reciprocal rather than imitative.

In terms of talk and partnership, the important function of the children's responses, along with their non-verbal behaviour gave the teachers and mothers enough flexibility in their roles to enable successful completion of the task. The teachers assumed that the children comprehended their utterances, however complex, and were unaware that their utterances grew longer at every move. Although the interactions were collaborative, the teachers dominated the moves and managed the content of the conversation by means of questions and evaluations. It was as though the teachers had to assess each of the children's utterances to make sure they were factually accurate and made sense.

At times, the teachers increased the complexity of what they said by taking very long and complex turns. Unlike the mother–child or grandmother–child interactions, the teachers seldom checked to ensure that they had correctly understood their partner in the activity before making the next move. The teachers were so concerned that the children should see the experience from their own adult perspective that they failed to pick up some of the cues from the children. In the case of Habib, for example, Jade changed the subject when he wanted to extend the conversation about cars, whereas the grandmothers accepted the ideas volunteered by the children and used them as a basis for collaboration in constructing a more extended understanding. Their utterances were listened to and the grandmothers shared their own experiences with their grandchildren to enrich their interactions.

The child as teacher

In their research with teacher partnerships between mainstream and complementary school teachers, Kenner and Ruby (2012) found that children liked to play the role of teacher, a strategy the complementary school teachers tended to use to support children's learning. In the questionnaires the grandmothers filled in for my study and that of Kenner *et al.* (2004a), they said the grandchildren liked role plays where they acted as the teacher. Gregory also found in her research among siblings (Gregory *et al.*, 2002) that children like to play teachers at home. My study also found that when the child was interacting with a novice, whether younger or older, they took on the role of the expert. With the teachers, they assumed the role of the novice. With their mothers they were expected to be novices, but they had the confidence to negotiate their role, as we saw. When they completed the puzzle activity with their grandmothers, they thrived in their role as the expert. The children directed their grandmothers on what to look for and how to fit the pieces together. They were also actively involved when they handed over the reins to their grandparents at the end of the activity, during which the grandmothers became the experts.

During the period of listening to, interpreting, and transcribing the video recordings, the following transcript of Samiha at home afforded new insights into the significance of the data. I was fascinated to see Samiha using words and tones with her grandmother and the children that sounded just like her teacher. The transcript is from the activity with her mother, when her first cousin, Akhter, and younger sister, Surayah, were present. Samiha took the initiative to involve everyone in the final discussion. She orchestrated the learning, by inviting Akhter into the circle, and skilfully involved him in the task of reflecting on the activity (turns 332 and 333). She also allowed her mother to play a part in the task by accepting her contributions and co-facilitating the discussion:

EXAMPLE 14 (Samiha–mother pair: S: Samiha, M: mother, Ak: Akhter, Su: Surayah)

332. S: Akhter do you want to help us?
333. S: come on here here here
334. ((S pats the floor next to her for her cousin to come and join her))
335. (...)
336. S: what sound does a lion make?
337. ((S asking Ak))
338. ((A makes the sound of a lion, which Su copies))
339. M: wow
340. (...)
341. M: what's that?
342. ((M points to another animal in the puzzle))
343. Ak: p-parrot
344. S: yees
345. M: parrot
346. (...)
347. M: look at that snake what colour is it?
348. Ak: ( ) and blue
349. M and S: yees
350. M: it's a very unusual colour

351. S: Surayah lion?
352. ((S points to the picture and makes the sound))
353. Su: lion here
354. ((Su points to a different animal))
355. M: that one is a lion
356. ((all the children make the sound of a lion while looking at the picture, and S laughs, looking up at the camera))
357. ((M laughs, puts her hands up in the air and makes the sound as well))
358. ((all the children laugh))
359. S: what colour are the top of the mountains?
360. Ak: white

The teacher-like character of the questions was evident in Samiha's interaction with Akhter and Surayah. We can also see the influence of Samiha's mother's teacher-like language.

416. S: Akhter can you tell me what this is?
417. ((S points to the picture))
418. ((Ak leans forward to get a closer look))
419. Ak: a monkey!
420. S: can you do the noise?
421. ((S looks at A))
422. Ak: yeah
423. ((S and Ak make the noises and the body gestures of a monkey))
424. S: ok this is water isn't it?
425. S: falling from the mountains
426. (.)
427. ((S looks towards Ak and back again))
428. S: falling from the mountain

Samiha asks questions that are direct, closed and rhetorical, following the style of teachers Hasna and Jade, and the mothers. She is very much taking the lead.

The findings parallel work by Gregory (1998), Gregory and Williams (2000), Gregory *et al.* (2002), Brooker (2002), Jessel *et al.* (2004) and Kenner *et al.* (2004b). The researchers recognize that parents and teachers may not be the most influential facilitators and consider the role played by siblings and grandparents in informal learning settings. With teachers, the children spoke less. They took fewer turns, expressed a narrower range of meanings, asked fewer questions, made fewer requests, and initiated a much smaller proportion of conversations. This was because the teachers initiated a much higher proportion of conversations than the parents and grandparents did. The initiator was normally the one who chose the topic in their turns. Teachers asked a higher proportion of questions, particularly questions that tested the children's knowledge. The result was that the children were reduced for far more of the time to the more passive role of respondent, trying to answer the teachers' many questions and complying with their requests.

The children sometimes played the teacher's role with their mothers and grandmothers and engaged in partnership to different degrees. The grandmothers enabled the novices to experiment with language and to rehearse and improve their repertoire by expanding their vocabulary base. In addition, they acted as socializing agents and 'cultural and linguistic mediators' (Volk and de Acosta, 2004). But unlike the grandmothers, the teachers and mothers introduced the less experienced learners to strategies such as paying attention, listening, practising, or evaluating their competences. Being put in the role of a less knowledgeable participant significantly reduced the level of competence shown by the children when they were interacting with the teachers. This was because the teachers assumed a more dominating role than the parents and grandparents during the conversations. The teachers incorporated only half as often the meanings offered by the children's utterances, either by extending those meanings or by inviting the children to extend their ideas themselves. Instead, they tended to develop the meanings they themselves had introduced into the conversations. This left the children with little to say, whereas their conversation skills were very apparent in their conversations with their mothers and grandmothers.

The next chapter brings together the findings from my research and explores their implications for parents, teachers, policy-makers, and others who are interested in promoting children's learning. What can they do to recognize, facilitate, and strengthen the skills of bilingual and multilingual children to be flexible learners?

Chapter 7

Learner flexibility and what this implies

> Our previous sense of knowledge, language and identity, our peculiar inheritance, cannot be simply rubbed out of the story, cancelled. What we have inherited – as culture, as history, as language, as tradition, as a sense of identity – is not destroyed but taken apart, opened up to questioning, rewriting, and re-routing.
>
> Chambers, 1994: 24

The study originally set out to attain greater understanding about the significance of intergenerational collaborative interactions and how these would impact on the children's learning. However, what has emerged and is discussed in this chapter is a more complex understanding of the process involved in learning in a sociocultural context. The evidence from my research data is that there are similarities but also significant differences in the interactions between the children, their families, and their teachers, and that these affect children's learning.

Three grandmothers, mothers, and grandchildren and two teachers took part in the study. By videotaping collaborative interactions and analysing them for moments of teaching and learning, I was able to delve deeper into the interactions, but also, importantly, into the new ways of communicating created by the adults and the children. Researchers have explored the constructs of peer and sibling interactions and some that are intergenerational, but they have not investigated the interactions within three-generation families and the benefits children receive from such exchanges. My research addressed this gap by exploring the cognitive and social aspects of intergenerational interactions and the value and impact of these experiences on the children involved.

Wells (2009) observed that children's development depends on opportunities to participate with members of their families, peers, and teachers in activities that are culturally meaningful within their social context. Rogoff (1990) also spoke about the relationships children have in their communities that allow them to experience the cultural world together and use the knowledge gained from those experiences to form their own beliefs, attitudes, and behaviours. Moll *et al.* (2013) call this informal learning, learning that builds children's funds of knowledge. The relationships between the children in this study and their different pairings in school and at home reveal important findings about the children's experiences as learners and the way they utilized these experiences to learn.

This book has sought not only to present the voices of Bangladeshi families living in the UK, but also to highlight the challenges third-generation British Bangladeshi children face in being recognized for their notable wealth of knowledge (Luke and Kale, 1997) that teachers can draw on to better their cognitive and social development. The contributions grandparents make to their grandchildren's learning complements and support the children's learning and extends it both socially and academically. The collaborative interactions shared in this book are based around the concepts of children's active participation in their development and the different roles they assumed in their learning. The crucial roles of the children in the interactions at school and at home demonstrated their learner flexibilities, a concept that has emerged from my research and characterizes the learner identities of these third-generation British-Bangladeshi children.

The interactions between the teachers and the children highlight a discontinuity between the way children learn in their everyday lives at home and how they learn in classroom settings. This book builds on findings from research by Drury (2007) and Kenner *et al.* (2008) that show how classroom interactions reflect mainly unidirectional transmission with scaffolding the main learning construct. Yet contemporary sociocultural views identify learning as a social and cultural process in which participation is interdependent.

The teachers involved in the collaborative interactions described here assisted the children to reach higher levels of performance, allowing them to perform at levels they could not have achieved on their own. However, although the end goal of completing the puzzle was achieved, the strategies the teachers used to implement scaffolding involved assuming authority and control, evident in the nature of questions asked and the pattern of turn-taking during the activity. This gave teachers the role of the more knowledgeable adult and the child the role of novice. The teachers' perceptions of the children's ability to share decisions were limited, as revealed by the nature of conversations between them. Tharp and Gallimore (1988) suggested teachers instruct learning by asking children specific questions that help them to see what they need to do next and to point to aspects of the task the children may have overlooked.

Nearly three decades later, the role of teachers has not changed: my findings also showed that across all the activities, the children tended to ask fewer questions and took fewer turns than the teachers, and the questions asked by the teachers were directed more to achieve completion of the activity than to allow the children to speak and contribute. Teachers asked mostly closed questions (Siraj-Blatchford and Manni, 2008) and did not give children enough time to respond to them.

It was also significant that Cazden's (1988) argument that teachers were not spending enough time learning about children's backgrounds, cultures, and families still pertains. The interviews with the teachers in my study revealed that they had little knowledge of the children's lives at home as learners or who they learned with there. Despite this, the children were not overtly disempowered by their experiences at school: they still managed to interact and take part in the activity. They adopted strategies to decide when to listen and comply and to speak when spoken to, thus showing their ability to manage the circumstances in which they are placed, thereby enabling the teachers to play their role as the knowledgeable adult.

The two teachers, although from different backgrounds, used similar patterns of interaction. Both based their interactions on a belief that their role in the process and achievement of the product was important. Intriguingly, even though one teacher was fully literate in Bengali and in tune with the cultural practices of the children, she did not use that resource in her role as a teacher during the activities. This supports the research by Kenner *et al.* (2008) that showed that bilingual teachers needed prompting and coaching to realize ways in which they could use their linguistic and cultural skills and knowledge in their classrooms. Children's learning experiences could have been much greater had the teachers used the opportunities to enrich the children's learning by welcoming and utilizing their existing knowledge. Children are active participants in a range of activities at home, but these resources or funds of knowledge of the children's world outside the classroom are rarely drawn on in school. Cultures and families differ in the ways in which they make sense of children's experiences and development. These differences are reflected in the ways in which parents, teachers, and grandparents interact with children, and these differences in children's early experiences must be taken into account by teachers and other adults within the school settings if children are to learn optimally.

The teachers can show appreciation of the children's funds of knowledge by taking the time to converse with them about their learning at home, who they learn with, what languages they speak at home and with whom, and what activities they are involved in outside school. This would show that the teachers are aware of the wealth of knowledge the children bring with them and the insight they gain would make the teaching and learning experiences more meaningful for all parties involved. The teacher would have a deeper understanding of children's emotional and cognitive behaviour, and this would help them become effective mediators in the learning of new skills (Gregory *et al.*, 2004).

Learner identity at home
Interaction with mothers
The process of guided participation between the children and their mothers highlights the teaching and learning strategies that exist within these guided experiences. The specific actions and communications that occurred between the participants and the nature of such interactions enabled the children to take on a more relaxed role with their mothers, and even more so with their grandmothers, than they did with their teachers. The mothers and children used verbal and non-verbal communication to observe and interact, creating a comfortable feeling between them during the interactions that allowed the children to explore and learn at their ease. The children were more interactive with their mothers than they were with their teachers, creating more opportunities to observe, ask questions, and give suggestions, which enabled them to create a collaborative experience, guiding each other's efforts. This, Rogoff (1991; Rogoff *et al.*, 1993) argued, is guided participation, where the children actively observe and participate in activities on a more equal footing.

The children felt at ease to ask more questions than they did with the teachers and to seek directions, also giving rise to more non-verbal communication such as hand gestures and gaze. The younger children who were present during a couple of the activities heard and observed their older siblings and mothers interacting, and felt encouraged to also join in. This supports Rogoff's (1990) observation that there are social and participatory implications when children observe others and that this can also contribute to cognitive growth as the interactions are structured with a process and goal.

The way in which the second-generation Bangladeshi mothers interacted with their children extends the knowledge gained from studies by Schieffelin (1990) and Heath (1982). They highlight the complex role second-generation women play in a context where they are mothers who have been exposed to the educational and social structures of their host community. Similar to middle-class British and American mothers (Schieffelin and Ochs, 1983), these three mothers facilitated dyadic conversations treating the children as communicative partners, but at times behaved like the

Roadville mothers (Heath, 1982), who tried to show the children how to talk by carefully choosing the language they conversed in. Like the children from Trackton (Heath, 1982), Aminah, Samiha, and Habib came home to an environment that included a lot of human contact and communication as well as several languages. They were exposed to the languages through different media including Bengali TV channels, newspapers, and bilingual books as well as their complementary classes (see Kenner *et al.*, 2004a).

Researchers, theorists, practitioners, and policy-makers would all agree that parents play a crucial role in the education of their children. Evidence comes from investigations into the practices organized by parents of monolingual (Heath, 1983; Schieffelin and Ochs, 1986b; Wells, 1986) and bilingual children (Gregory and Penman, 1983; Drury, 2007). Although the teachers in this and other research studies hold views of parents as poorly informed, lacking expertise, and needing help in supporting their children to learn, my study shows that all three parents were very interested in their children's academic development and in tune with school structures – so much so that they took on the role of teachers at home. They also felt they were well equipped to guide their children through their academic lives. The mothers resembled the American caregivers in Rogoff *et al.*'s study (1993), acting as both teachers and playmates with their children during the puzzle activities. The mothers, Layla, Shamima, and Thaminah like those in Rogoff *et al.*'s later study (1998), structured their children's participation so that opportunities were created for them to be involved and supported. They did this in two ways, firstly by involving the grandparents in the lives of the children, and secondly by sending the children to complementary classes where they were intellectually challenged and the roles they were given were in line with those valued in their community.

Interaction with grandmothers

This book contributes to a new line of thinking by clarifying why considering grandparents, parents, and children simultaneously as a three-generational family system is so valuable. The powerful connection it highlights between the children and their grandmothers has been largely overlooked by researchers. Only one other study in this field – that by Kenner *et al.* (2004b) – has been carried out from a sociocultural perspective. The role of grandparents as caregivers in times of difficulty is still an area that is researched and the findings are a strong predictor of the quality of grandparent–grandchild relationships. However, the general caregiving bonds described in this book have far-reaching implications within families that are not facing difficulties. The traditional assumption that mothers and grandmothers fulfil most of the inter-family relationships in multigenerational families is extended in this study to demonstrate the influence they have on the cognitive and social development of children, building on the study by Kenner *et al.*

When considering the role of grandmothers in the lives of their grandchildren, there is evidence of transmission of knowledge identified by Cole (1996) as the process of prolepsis. The examples of prolepsis apparent here are the maintenance of the Bengali language, of faith, and of cultural knowledge. The grandmothers all demonstrated the importance of the heritage language by speaking mainly in Bengali with the grandchildren and using the puzzle as an opportunity to encourage and coax them to interact in Bengali. Acculturation is clear: both the mothers and grandmothers have adapted their styles of interaction with the children to include teacher-like behaviour and speech, as well as drawing on their own experiences from their cultures (Gregory *et al.*, 2004).

The children in this study were actively involved in the activities with their mothers and grandmothers, and these contrasted with the children's experiences with their teachers. However, with the grandmothers we see an added layer of ease that allowed the children to function within the zone of proximal development, which Gregory (2001) associates with synergy. Synergy is also evidenced by grandmothers and grandchildren having reciprocity in their interactions, teaching each other, and learning in the process. The obvious comfort between the children and grandmothers in the interactions I observed existed because the grandmothers established an environment that allowed the children to explore and learn freely and also because each used the other as a teaching and learning guide. The children and grandmothers observed each other's actions and manipulations, asked questions to define ideas or motivations, and built on each other's expressions and actions to create a more intricate and collaborative experience.

The experiences of putting the puzzle pieces together required the children to listen to their grandmothers and follow one another's cues in order to progress the task. The grandmothers coordinated their ideas together with the children to create a more involving process for the activity, sometimes acting as orchestrators (Ruby *et al.*, 2010) enabling all to take part in the activity. The relaxed atmosphere also allowed the participants to communicate their choices of moves and support each other's development throughout the process as collaborators. Rogoff *et al.* (2001) described interactions of this kind as opportunities where children move from their current understanding to a higher level through their communications with fellow participants. This bidirectional relationship allowed the children to take on the role of teacher and learner, which did not happen with the teacher or mothers. We see them taking this teacher role when they communicated with their grandmothers in a reciprocal manner, treating them as learners. The children expressed their knowledge verbally, asked more questions, and shared their ideas in a directive and exploratory tone. They also received input from others present during the activities through listening or observing.

Reciprocity (Gregory, 2001) and mutuality (Kenner *et al.*, 2007) also existed in the interactions between the grandmothers and the children, where each offered the other adjusted support in their explorations as they became more comfortable. This collaborative experience for the children is different from being taught, as it consists of mutual involvement with a certain equality in the relationship and motivation based on a shared understanding. Vygotsky argued that collaboration could not occur unless the children had a shared understanding or 'intersubjectivity' (Rogoff, 1990; Rommetveit, 1988; Trevarthen, 1979). A shared understanding is achieved through constant communication and reciprocation between the participants. The presence of intersubjectivity in each interaction enhanced the experience for the children by allowing them to share their ideas and skills when they took on a teacher role and at the same time attain new knowledge and skills from their grandmothers when they took on a learner role.

Throughout the puzzle activities, the children actively negotiated their ideas and made their intentions known to their grandmothers as they put the puzzle pieces together. Through such expression and negotiation, the children developed insights about new and creative ways to further their experiences – what Gregory calls syncretism – melding different cultural practices (Gregory *et al.*, 2004). When interacting with their grandmothers at home, all three children exhibited their ability to code-switch, and rehearsed some of the cultural aspects of being a student and a teacher in an English school by readily emulating their teachers during the activity. All three children are purposeful in creating continuity from their learning experiences at school to their home contexts, where they participate in lively exchanges centred on family experiences, thus demonstrating their ability to practise and play with their language ability and develop their language competence and confidence. We also see the children's attempts to teach their grandmothers English during their interactions.

These interactions also gave rise to opportunities for the grandmothers to use the presence of the children to increase their understanding of their social world. Rogoff (1990) suggested that peer interactions give children the opportunity to practise and extend ideas, participate in role relations, and observe more skilled peers as well as adults as being resources. I believe the intergenerational interactions with grandmothers fulfilled similar purposes. These interactions also gave rise to syncretic learning practices where grandmothers and children found new ways to learn. The grandmothers used the completed puzzles to share experiences, decisions, and responsibilities during the activity, as well as aspects of their lives, and this created a socially supportive and culturally responsive context in which they could learn together. Findings from this study reveal the importance of providing opportunities for children to take responsibility and to share decision-making during activities.

Learner flexibility and implications for practitioners

I define a new approach to the way bilingual and multilingual children function as learners; their ability to engage at different levels with different adults I define as their skill at being 'flexible learners'. The children transformed their participation as they engaged with different adults in a way that has implications for practitioners. Given the opportunity to participate in a wide range of roles during their interactions, the children established new identities, consciously knowing when to ask questions, when to listen, when to engage with the ideas of others and reach new understandings. When they had the opportunity with their grandmothers, the children moved beyond seeing themselves as empty vessels to seeing themselves as learners with others as knowledge-builders who co-constructed new understandings. Participating in this way afforded them 'texture to negotiate identities' (Wenger, 1998: 269). The experiences of the three children at home described in this book reveal the funds of knowledge that go unrecognized by their school teachers and at times by their mothers. Their effects are hard to measure, but children's educational progress could be held back if funds of knowledge are not recognized and enhanced, as is clear from the research by Kenner *et al.* (2007). The children have developed a learner's flexibility as a means of 'finding their way' (Drury, 2013) through the activities.

Figure 7.1 highlights the relationships and connections between the children and the adults. It exhibits the connections that support the children at the centre to develop skills, consciously and through experience, and become flexible learners when their funds of knowledge are the bedrock of all interactions. The child at the centre has strong links with each of the adults and also shows the main learner construct that is involved in the interactions between each of the relationships (scaffolding with teachers, guided participation with mothers, and synergy with grandmothers). The learning construct of prolepsis is present within the space of the home. The diagram suggests that the link between the teacher and the mother is weak or partial and the link between mother and grandmother is strong. However, currently there are no links between the school and the grandparents and this gap between home and school and the lack of recognition of how, what, and with whom the children learn impacts on the relationships of all concerned. It can also affect the children's learning. The child acquires skills from their many interactions within school and at home, but the latter have yet to be recognized by practitioners. The quote from Chambers (1994) that opens this chapter reflects the findings from my study. The 'previous sense of knowledge, language and identity, our peculiar inheritance' from the grandparents 'cannot be simply rubbed out of the story, cancelled'. The parents' generation has a 'peculiar inheritance' that manifests 'as culture, as history, as language, as tradition, as a sense of identity'. It forms part of the process of prolepsis taking place, which is then passed on to the next generations. The third-generation children demonstrate that what is passed on 'is not destroyed but taken apart, opened up to questioning, rewriting, and re-routing' through the syncretic learning experiences that take place between the generations as they explore new kinds of interactions.

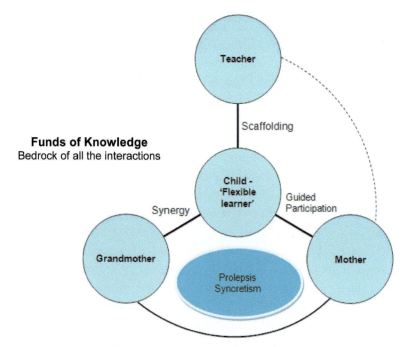

Figure 7.1: Interconnected relationships between the children and adults

Each connection for these multilingual children enables them to develop a set of skills and strategies that support them in their simultaneous and often multiple worlds to understand their role in each world. From the findings of this study it is clear that it is the children who are at the centre of these interactions: they acquire funds of knowledge that are rich and diverse. They are in a position to juggle their fused knowledge and develop awareness to judge when they need to fulfil the role of the learner or the role of the giver of knowledge, sometimes playing both roles at once. The relationship between the mothers and grandmothers in this study is strong and highlights the importance of the transmission of language, cultural, and faith knowledge from one generation to another.

The children are enriched by the existence of prolepsis, which Cole (1996: 183) explains from a sociocultural perspective as 'the cultural mechanism that brings the end into the beginning'. As one generation passes on its values and skills, the next generation transforms them into another set of values and skills shaped by their own experiences. This leads to syncretic forms of learning for these children due to their responsiveness and liveliness as well as the fact that they use Bengali and English confidently within the home setting. The importance of using Bengali is that it allows the children to practise, rehearse, and play with language when interacting with their siblings and grandparents. The guided participation and the existence of synergy within the interactions at home enable the children to understand and appreciate the roles they can play as learners and teachers.

The acquisition of faith and culture is extended for the children when they enter school and are exposed to many more cultures and faiths. However, in my study and others, the children leave some of their funds of knowledge at the school gates because the teachers don't call upon them. Here the children learn to listen and comply, consciously and skilfully enabling the teacher to feel they can transmit their knowledge and skills to the children and perform the role of the more knowledgeable adult. However, what the children did do was demonstrate that they can bring the knowledge they acquire at school to the home context. The mothers also demonstrated this when they took on the role of teacher with their children during the activities, drawing on their own experiences of being schooled in the UK. The children's ability to be flexible learners can be recognized and appreciated if the link between the school and family can be strengthened beyond parent–teacher meetings and if a link can at last be formed with the grandparents.

When children were afforded active roles during the interactions I observed, they became more interested in their learning, particularly when learning became personally meaningful and culturally relevant. There was a noticeable increase in the children's confidence to share their learning and value the importance of learning together. The book describes research that illustrates the extraordinary resolve the children have in making the most of their interactions and building on their skills and knowledge base. It is important to recognize that, although the teachers, mothers, and grandmothers may have had definite plans and were willing to assist the children in their learning, the children emerge as key players in coping with the linguistic and cultural demands imposed on them, ultimately finding ways to mediate and take ownership of their own learning. Practitioners and family members need to recognize and celebrate the extraordinary journeys multilingual children embark on in the challenge of succeeding in linguistically and culturally different educational environments.

There are implications for practitioners from these findings. Teachers, parents, educators, and policy-makers must give more attention to multilingual children who are fluent in their host language and are doing well at school academically and socially. Recognizing their language skills and abilities as flexible learners will allow children to be stretched and achieve still more, cognitively and socially.

There are many ways to achieve this. Ideas such as grandparents' coffee mornings, sending tasks home with children that require interaction with members of the extended family in different languages, and classroom interaction promoting the discussion of work in different languages can be developed at school by practitioners and implemented in the classroom. The teachers who made learner visits to homes (Cremin *et al.*, 2015) and community classes extended their own funds of knowledge through 'asking respectful questions and by learning to listen and look with a researcher's gaze – with a willingness and openness to learn more about others' (Mottram and Powell, 2015: 144). This transformed the way the teachers embedded their learning in their classrooms to enhance children's learning.

There are two broad conclusions: firstly, from a sociological perspective, intergenerational learning between grandparents and their grandchildren extends the concepts from sociocultural theories of learning, guided participation, and scaffolding. The concepts of synergy, syncretizing of knowledge from different sources, and prolepsis take on new meaning as the children and their grandmothers each bring to their interactions funds of knowledge that are unique and meaningful – in the case of my research – to building the child's learner identity of being a bilingual British Bangladeshi.

Secondly, from a policy, education, and community perspective, the research points to ways in which policy-makers, Bangladeshi parents, community leaders, and professionals working with Bangladeshi children can facilitate the maintenance of children's bilinguality as they journey from home–to–school–to–home. Teachers, educators, and policy-makers in particular need to become more aware of the socio-political climate in which young children in inner city areas such as Tower Hamlets are growing up. They do not live in a vacuum, but are part of an interconnected social context, living in simultaneous worlds. Young children carry the different jigsaw pieces of their identities with them as they enter and leave different spaces. The educational world is intertwined with the children's social world. So schools need to value the role of the parents and also the grandparents and to recognize the importance of the culture and languages the children bring with them. Finally, I stress the crucial role teachers and bilingual teaching assistants can play in acknowledging and furthering the development of the bilingual child's learner flexibility within the classroom.

References

Adler, P.A., and Adler, P. (1987) *Membership Roles in Field Research*. Newbury Park, CA: Sage.

Al-Azami, S. (2006) *The Silver Lining of My Life. Learning with grandparents: A report of the work of the National Development Project 2005–2006*. Nottingham: Basic Skills Agency.

Apter, A. (1991) 'Herkovits's heritage: Rethinking syncretism in the African diaspora'. *Diaspora: A Journal of Transnational Studies*, 1 (3), 35–260.

Asselin, M.E. (2003) 'Insider research: Issues to consider when doing qualitative research in your own setting'. *Journal for Nurses in Staff Development*, 19 (2), 99–103.

Basic Skills Agency (2007) www.basic-skills.co.uk

Bateson, G. (1979) *Mind and Nature: A necessary unity*. London: Wildwood House.

Berk, L.E., and Winsler, A. (1995) *Scaffolding Children's Learning: Vygotsky and early childhood education* (NAEYC Research into Practice Series 7). Washington, DC: NAEYC.

Bourdieu, P. (1977) *Outline of a Theory of Practice*. Trans. Nice, R. Cambridge: Cambridge University Press.

Brooker, L. (2002) *Starting School: Young children learning cultures*. Buckingham: Open University Press.

Bruner, J. (1984) 'Interaction, communication and self'. *Journal of the American Academy of Child Psychiatry*, 23 (1), 17.

Cazden, C. (1971) 'Evaluation of learning in preschool education: Early language development'. In Bloom, B.S., Hastings, T., and Medaus, G. (eds) *Handbook on Formative and Summative Evaluation of Student Learning*. New York: McGraw Hill, 345–98.

— (1988) *Classroom Discourse: The language of teaching and learning*. Portsmouth, NH: Heinemann.

Chambers, I. (1994) *Migrancy, Culture, Identity*. London and New York: Routledge.

Cole, M. (1996) *Cultural Psychology: A once and future discipline*. Cambridge, MA: Harvard University Press.

Cremin, T., and Collins, F.M. (2015) 'Introduction: Setting the context'. In Cremin, T., Mottram, M., Collins, F.M., Powell, S., and Drury, R., *Researching Literacy Lives: Building communities between home and school*. London: Routledge.

Cremin, T., and Drury, R. (2015) 'Laying the foundations'. In Cremin, T., Mottram, M., Collins, F.M., Powell, S., and Drury, R., *Researching Literacy Lives: Building communities between home and school*. London: Routledge.

Cremin, T., Mottram, M., Collins, F.M., Powell, S., and Drury, R. (2015) *Researching Literacy Lives: Building communities between home and school*. London: Routledge.

Crozier, G., and Davies, J. (2007) 'Hard to reach parents or hard to reach schools? A discussion of home–school relations, with particular reference to Bangladeshi and Pakistani parents'. *British Educational Research Journal*, 33 (3), 295–313.

Crystal, D. (1987) *Child Language, Learning, and Linguistics*. London: E. Arnold. Cited in Brown, A. (2009) *Developing Language and Literacy 3–8*. London: Sage.

Cummins, J. (1996) *Negotiating Identities: Education for empowerment in a diverse society*. Ontario, CA: California Association for Bilingual Education.

— (2006) 'Identity texts: The imaginative construction of self through multiliteracies pedagogy'. In García, O., Skutnabb-Kangas, T., and Torres-Guzmán, M.E. (eds) *Imagining Multilingual Schools*. Clevedon: Multilingual Matters, 51–68.

Drew, L.M. (2000) 'What are the implications for grandparents when they lose contact with their grandchildren?' Ph.D. diss., Goldsmiths, University of London.

Drury, R. (2003) 'Young bilingual children learning at home and at school'. Ph.D. diss., Goldsmiths, University of London.

— (2007) *Young Bilingual Learners at Home and School: Researching multilingual voices*. Stoke-on-Trent: Trentham Books.

— (2013) 'How silent is the "Silent Period" for young bilinguals in early years settings in England?' *European Early Childhood Education Research Journal*, 21 (3), 380–91.

Duranti, A., and Ochs, E. (1997) 'Syncretic literacy in a Samoan American family'. In Resnick, L.B., Säljö, R., Pontecorvo, C., and Burge, B. (eds) *Discourse, Tools, and Reasoning: Essays on situated cognition*. Berlin: Springer Verlag.

Edwards, V. (1998) *The Power of Babel: Teaching and learning in multilingual classrooms*. Stoke-on-Trent: Trentham Books.

Fay, B. (1996) *Contemporary Philosophy of Social Science: A multicultural approach*. Cambridge: Blackwell.

Gauvain, M. (2001) *The Social Context of Cognitive Development*. New York: Guilford Press.

González, N., Moll, L., and Amanti, C. (eds) (2005) *Funds of Knowledge: Theorizing practices in households, communities, and classrooms*. Mahwah, NJ: Lawrence Erlbaum Associates.

Gregory, E. (1994) 'Cultural assumptions and early years' pedagogy: The effect of home culture on minority children's interpretation of reading in school'. *Language, Culture and Curriculum*, 7 (2), 111–24.

— (1998) 'Siblings as mediators of literacy in linguistic minority communities'. *Language and Education*, 12 (1), 33–55.

— (2001) 'Sisters and brothers as language and literacy teachers: Synergy between siblings playing and working together'. *Journal of Early Childhood Literacy*, 1 (3), 301–22.

Gregory, E., Arju, T., Jessel, J., Kenner, C., and Ruby, M. (2007) 'Snow White in different guises: Interlingual and intercultural exchanges between grandparents and young children at home in East London'. *Journal of Early Childhood Literacy*, 7 (1), 5–25.

Gregory, E., Long, S., and Volk, D. (eds) (2004) *Many Pathways to Literacy: Young children learning with siblings, grandparents, peers and communities*. London: RoutledgeFalmer.

Gregory, E., and Penman, D. (1983) 'Investigating the potential of the mother tongue in school'. *English in Education*, 17, 48–55.

Gregory, E., and Williams, A. (2000) *City Literacies: Learning to read across generations and cultures*. London: Routledge.

Gyllenspetz, I. (2007) *Learning with Grandparents: Trialling the materials*. Leicester: Basic Skills Agency at NIACE.

Hammersley, M., and Atkinson, P. (1993) *Ethnography: Principles in practice*. London: Routledge.

Harkness, S. (1975) 'Cultural variations in mother's language'. In Raffler-Engel, W. von (ed.) *Child Language 1975*. Special ed. *Word*, 27, 495–8.

Harkness, S., and Super, C.M. (1977) 'Why African children are so hard to test'. In Adler, L.L. (ed.) *Issues in Cross-cultural Research* (Annals of the New York Academy of Sciences 285), 326–31.

— (1992) 'Parental ethnotheories in action'. In Sigel, I.E., McGillicuddy-De Lisi, A.V., and Goodnow, J.J. (eds) *Parental Belief System: The psychological consequences for children*. 2nd ed. Hillsdale, NJ: Lawrence Erlbaum Associates.

Heath, S.B. (1980) 'The functions and uses of literacy'. *Journal of Communication*, 29 (2), 123–33.

— (1982) 'What no bedtime story means: Narrative skills at home and school'. *Language in Society*, 11 (2), 49–76.

— (1983) *Ways with Words: Language, life, and work in communities and classrooms*. Cambridge: Cambridge University Press.

— (1991) 'The sense of being literate: Historical and cross-cultural features'. In Barr, R., Kamil, M.L., Mosenthal, P., and Pearson, P.D. (eds) *Handbook of Reading Research*, vol. 2. New York: Longman, 3–25.

Holton, D., and Clarke, D. (2006) 'Scaffolding and metacognition'. *International Journal of Mathematical Education in Science and Technology*, 37 (2), 127–43.

Hymes, D. (1974) 'Ways of speaking'. In Bauman, R., and Sherzer, J. (eds) *Explorations in the Ethnography of Speaking*. Cambridge: Cambridge University Press, 433–51.

Isaacson, D. (2010) *42 Thinking Skills You Can Learn from Doing Jigsaw Puzzles*. Online. http://tinyurl.com/7a23vwt [Last accessed 28 October 2016].

Jefferson, G. (1984) 'Transcript Notation'. In Atkinson, J., and Heritage, J. (eds) *Structures of Social Interaction*. New York: Cambridge University Press.

Jessel, J., Arju, T., Gregory, E., Kenner, C., and Ruby, M. (2004) 'Children and their grandparents at home: A mutually supportive context for learning and linguistic development'. *English Quarterly*, 36 (4), 16–23.

Kanuha, V.K. (2000) '"Being" native versus "going native": Conducting social work research as an insider'. *Social Work*, 45 (5), 439–47.

Kelly, C., Gregory, E., and Williams, A. (2002) 'Developing literacy: Towards a new understanding of family involvement'. In Fisher, R., Brooks, G., and Lewis, M. (eds) *Raising Standards in Literacy*. London: RoutledgeFalmer.

Kelly, J.B. (2004) 'Family mediation research: Is there empirical support for the field?' *Conflict Resolution Quarterly*, 22 (1–2), 3–35.

Kenner, C. (2004) *Becoming Biliterate: Young children learning different writing systems*. Stoke-on-Trent: Trentham Books.

Kenner, C., Arju, T., Gregory, E., Jessel, J., and Ruby, M. (2004a) 'The role of grandparents in children's learning'. *Primary Practice*, 38, 41–4.

Kenner, C., Gregory, E., and Jessel, J. (2004b) *Intergenerational learning between children and grandparents in East London*. ESRC Award R000220131 (2003–4) final report.

Kenner, C., Gregory, E., Ruby, M., and Al-Azami, S. (2008) 'Bilingual learning for second and third-generation children'. *Language, Culture and Curriculum*, 21 (2), 120–37.

Kenner, C., and Ruby, M. (2012) *Interconnecting Worlds: Teacher partnerships for bilingual learning*. Stoke-on-Trent: Trentham Books.

Kenner, C., Ruby, M., Jessel, J., Gregory, E., and Arju, T. (2007) 'Intergenerational learning between children and grandparents in East London'. *Journal of Early Childhood Research*, 5 (3), 219–43.

King, V., and Elder, G.H. (1995) 'American children view their grandparents: Linked lives across three rural generations'. *Journal of Marriage and Family*, 57 (1), 165–78.

King, V., Russell, S.T., and Elder, G.H. (1998) 'Grandparenting in family systems: An ecological perspective'. In Szinovacz, M.E. (ed.) *Handbook on Grandparenthood*. Westport, CT: Greenwood Press, 53–69.

Kornhaber, A., and Woodward, K.L. (1981) *Grandparents/Grandchildren: The vital connection*. Garden City, NY: Anchor Press/Doubleday.

Kulick, D. (1992) *Language Shift and Cultural Reproduction: Socialization, self, and syncretism in a Papua New Guinean village*. Cambridge: Cambridge University Press.

Luke, A., and Kale, J. (1997) 'Learning through difference: Cultural practices in early language socialisation'. In Gregory, E. (ed.) *One Child, Many Worlds: Early learning in multi-cultural communities*. London: David Fulton Publishers.

Mahon, M. (1997) 'Conversational interactions between young deaf children and their families in homes where English is not the first language'. Ph.D. diss., University College London.

Moll, L. (1992) 'Bilingual classroom studies and community analysis: Some recent trends'. *Educational Researcher*, 21 (2), 20–4.

Moll, L.C., and Cammarota, C. (2010) 'Cultivating new funds of knowledge through research and practice'. In Dunsmore, K., and Fisher, D. (eds) *Bringing Literacy Home*. Newark, DE: International Reading Association.

Moll, L.C., Sáez, R., and Dworin, J. (2001) 'Exploring biliteracy: Two student case examples of writing as a social practice'. *The Elementary School Journal*, 101 (4), 435–49.

Moll, L.C., Soto-Santiago, S.L., and Schwartz, L. (2013) 'Funds of knowledge in changing communities'. In Hall, K., Cremin, T., Comber, B., and Moll, L.C. (eds) *International Handbook of Research on Children's Literacy, Learning, and Culture*. London: Wiley, 172–83.

Mottram, M., and Powell, S. (2015) 'Shifting perspectives about parents and children'. In Cremin, T., Mottram, M., Collins, F.M., Powell, S., and Drury, R., *Researching Literacy Lives: Building communities between home and school*. London: Routledge.

Murphy, P., and Wolfenden, F. (2013) 'Developing a pedagogy of mutuality in a capability approach: Teachers' experiences of using the Open Educational Resources (OER) of the teacher education in sub-Saharan Africa (TESSA) programme'. *International Journal of Educational Development*, 33 (3), 263–71.

Neugarten, B.L., and Weinstein, K.K. (1964) 'The changing American grandparent'. *Journal of Marriage and Family*, 26 (2), 199–204.

Richardson, L. (1990) 'Narrative and sociology'. *Journal of Contemporary Ethnography*, 19 (1), 116–35.

Rogoff, B. (1990) *Apprenticeship in Thinking: Cognitive development in social context*. New York: Oxford University Press.

— (1991) 'Social interaction as apprenticeship in thinking: Guided participation in spatial planning'. In Resnick, L.B., Levine, J.M., and Teasley, S.D. (eds) *Perspectives on Socially Shared Cognition*. Washington, DC: American Psychological Association, 349–64.

Rogoff, B., Goodman Turkanis, C., and Bartlett, L. (2001) *Learning Together: Children and adults in a school community*. New York: Oxford University Press.

Rogoff, B., Mistry, J., Göncü, A., and Mosier, C. (1993) *Guided Participation in Cultural Activity by Toddlers and Caregivers* (Monographs of the Society for Research in Child Development No. 236), 58 (7).

Rogoff, B., Mosier, C., Mistry, C., and Göncü, A. (1998) 'Toddlers' guided participation with their caregivers in cultural activity'. In Woodhead, M., Faulkner, D., and Littleton, K. (eds) *Cultural Worlds of Early Childhood*. London: Routledge, 225–49.

Rommetveit, R. (1988) 'On literacy and the myth of literal meaning'. In Saljo, R. (ed.) *The Written World: Studies in literate thought and action*. Berlin: de Gruyter, 13–40.

Rosaldo, R. (1993) *Culture and Truth: The remaking of social analysis*. Boston: Beacon Press.

Ruby, M. (2015) 'Family Jigsaws: Intergenerational learning between grandmothers, mothers and children in Bangladeshi families in East London'. Ph.D. diss., Goldsmiths, University of London.

Ruby, M., Gregory, E., Kenner, C., and Al-Azami, S. (2010) 'Grandmothers as orchestrators of early language and literacy lessons'. In Lytra, V., and Martin, P. (eds) *Sites of Multilingualism: Complementary schools in Britain today*. Stoke-on-Trent: Trentham Books, 57–68.

Ruby, M., Kenner, C., Jessel, J., Gregory, E., and Arju, T. (2007) 'Gardening with grandparents: An early engagement with the science curriculum'. *Early Years*, 27 (2), 131–44.

Schieffelin, B.B. (1990) *The Give and Take of Everyday Life: Language socialization of Kaluli children* (Studies in the Social and Cultural Foundations of Languages 9). Cambridge: Cambridge University Press.

Schieffelin, B.B., and Ochs, E. (1983) 'A cultural perspective on the transition from pre-linguistic to linguistic communication'. In Golinkoff, R. (ed.) *The Transition from Pre-Linguistic to Linguistic Communication*. Hillsdale, NJ: Lawrence Erlbaum Associates.

— (eds) (1986a) '*Language socialization*'. *Annual Review of Anthropology*, 15, 163–91.

— (eds) (1986b) *Language Socialization Across Cultures* (Studies in the Social and Cultural Foundations of Languages 3). New York: Cambridge University Press.

Shahed, S.M. (1993) 'Bengali folk rhymes: An introduction'. *Asian Folklore Studies*, 52, 143–60.

Shaw, R., and Stewart, C. (1994) 'Introduction: Problematising syncretism'. In Stewart, C., and Shaw, R. (eds) *Syncretism/Antisyncretism: The politics of religious synthesis*. London: Routledge, 1–24.

Siraj-Blatchford, I., and Manni, L. (2008) '"Would you like to tidy up now?" An analysis of adult questioning in the English Foundation Stage'. *Early Years*, 28 (1), 5–22.

Smith, P.K. (1995) 'Grandparenthood'. In Bornstein, M.H. (ed.) *Handbook of Parenting. Volume 3: Being and becoming a parent*. Mahwah, NJ: Lawrence Erlbaum Associates, 89–111.

Smyth, G. (2003) *Helping Bilingual Pupils to Access the Curriculum*. London: David Fulton Publishers.

Stone, C.A. (1998) 'The metaphor of scaffolding: Its utility for the field of learning disabilities'. *Journal of Learning Disabilities*, 31 (4), 344–64.

Tharp, R.G. (1994) 'Intergroup differences among Native Americans in socialization and child cognition: An ethnogenetic analysis'. In Greenfield, P.M., and Cocking, R.R. (eds) *Cross-Cultural Roots of Minority Child Development*. Hillsdale, NJ: Lawrence Erlbaum Associates, 87–105.

Tharp, R.G., and Gallimore, R. (1988) *Rousing Minds to Life: Teaching, learning, and schooling in social context*. Cambridge: Cambridge University Press.

Tinsley, B.R., and Parke, R.D. (1984) 'Grandparents as support and socialization agents'. In Lewes, M. (ed.) *Beyond the Dyad*. New York: Plenum, 161–94.

Tizard, B., and Hughes, M. (2002) *Young Children Learning*. Malden, MA: Blackwell.

Trevarthen, C. (1979) 'Communication and cooperation in early infancy: A description of primary intersubjectivity'. In Bullowa, M. (ed.) *Before Speech: The beginning of interpersonal communication*. Cambridge: Cambridge University Press.

Volk, D., and de Acosta, M. (2004) 'Mediating networks for literacy learning: The role of Puerto Rican siblings'. In Gregory, E., Long, S., and Volk, D. (eds) *Many Pathways to Literacy: Young children learning with siblings, grandparents, peers and communities*. London: RoutledgeFalmer, 25–39.

Vollmer, H. (1937) 'The Grandmother: A problem in child-rearing'. *American Journal of Orthopsychiatry*, 7, 378–82.

Vygotsky, L.S. (1978) *Mind in Society: The development of higher psychological processes*. Cambridge, MA: Harvard University Press.

Wells, C.G. (1986) *The Meaning Makers: Children learning language and using language to learn*. Portsmouth, NH: Heinemann.

— (2009) 'The social context of language and literacy development'. In Barbarin, O.A., Frome, P., and Marie-Winn, D. (eds) *The Handbook of Child Development and Early Education*. London: Sage, 271–302.

Wenger, E. (1998) *Communities of Practice: Learning, meaning, and identity*. Cambridge: Cambridge University Press.

Wertsch, J.V. (1985) *Vygotsky and the Social Formation of Mind*. Cambridge, MA: Harvard University Press.

Williams, A., and Nussbaum, J.F. (2001) *Intergenerational Communication Across the Lifespan*. Mahwah, NJ: Lawrence Erlbaum Associates.

Wood, D., Bruner, J.S., and Ross, G. (1976) 'The role of tutoring in problem solving'. *Journal of Child Psychology and Psychiatry*, 17, 89–100.

Index